BREAKFAST COOKBOOK

JULIA ROSS

Copyright © 2021

CONTENTS

WHAT IS BREAKFAST?

It is the most important meal of the day because the first after the long night fast. It has the role of replenishing all losses, including energy losses, which occurred during the night and provide the necessary nutrients to face the morning. Furthermore, it has been scientifically demonstrated that if the first meal is complete and balanced, one will instinctively choose the following meals in a more balanced and healthy way.

IS BREAKFAST THE SAME IN THE HOT AND COLD SEASONS?

During very hot summers, paradoxically, breakfast could be richer than that of winter, as in the early hours of the morning, when the temperature is not too high yet, you can eat with more appetite than the rest of the day.

DOES BREAKFAST ALWAYS HAVE TO BE THE SAME OR CHANGED EVERY DAY?

The important thing is that at least the two food groups milk / yogurt and cereals are always present. By varying the source of cereals (bread, rusks, cereal flakes, biscuits, etc.) and the integration of simple sugars (honey, jams), many diversified menus can be obtained. Variety always benefits dietary balance, even at breakfast. But, even if you prefer a breakfast that is always the same every day, if it is balanced in its components, that's fine anyway, better a breakfast that is always the same than not having breakfast!

SWEET OR SAVORY BREAKFAST?

The important thing is that you like breakfast: if you like something salty you have to try to indulge this desire. If the child likes a piece of cheese for breakfast, he can be satisfied from time to time, and if so, he can skip the milk, keeping the cereal portion instead.

WHAT ARE THE MISTAKES MADE AT BREAKFAST?

Especially in Italy, breakfast is often skipped. Another mistake is to make too much sugar at breakfast (e.g. fruit juice and snacks) and / or neglect the consumption of milk or yogurt.

STAY HEALTHY WITH BREAKFAST

With a healthy breakfast you can counteract obesity, diabetes and cardiovascular diseases. Prepare yourself a healthy, nutritious breakfast. This will prevent you from reaching for fast food, cigarettes and alcohol. Not eating breakfast leads to food cravings throughout the day.

MORNING DRINKS

During the night, the body loses almost its entire fluid reservoir. It is therefore important to replenish your fluid supply in the morning.

It is best to drink a glass or two of water, tea or freshly squeezed juice in the morning. This is how you increase your performance for the coming day.

Coffee doesn't do much for your fluid balance in the morning. We'll show you what it's all about in another tip.

HAVE BREAKFAST OR NOT?

Whether or not you want to have breakfast in the morning is entirely up to you. Not everyone can eat something right after getting up in the morning. It is advisable to prepare a small breakfast and take it with you to work or school. There it can then be eaten at any time.

For breakfast you can have porridge, a cereal, whole grain bread with avocado or a vegan breakfast. Fruits such as bananas or apples should not be missing in the morning.

WHY IS BREAKFAST IMPORTANT FOR OUR HEALTH?

1. Breakfast gives us energy for the day

The breakfast is known to be the most important meal of the day because it follows a fasting period of 8 to 12 hours (overnight). It must therefore be sufficient to meet our energy needs for the first part of the day to give us the strength to last until the midday meal.

Thus, the absence of breakfast can be manifested by a state of fatigue or even problems with concentration, as we will see in the next point.

2. It improves concentration and memory

During the night, the level of glucose (sugar) in the blood drops, our organs (especially organs which can only function with glucose as fuel - example: the brain) then function less well because they do not receive enough energy to be able to function properly, which is why we lack energy in the morning.

Studies show that children who eat breakfast before school are in better mental shape during the morning: their memory is Best Quality Re, creativity or their concentration is too, unlike the children not taking grandson lunch which then show more concentration or memorization problems. (This observation is also valid for adults: eating breakfast allows you to be more productive in the morning.)

Eating breakfast therefore gives us the "strength" necessary to attack the morning - thus enabling us to think clearly, to learn or to work.

3. Less risk of deficiencies

Breakfast is an opportunity for your body to receive nutrients that are essential for your body to function. People who skip breakfast will be at greater risk of deficiency in the long run, especially if their diet for the rest of the day is unbalanced.

4. It prevents snacking

If you start the day on an empty stomach, you will probably feel a little hungry during the morning which may distract you or even lead you to snack.

However, lacks of bowl, the things that nibble away from meals are often the least balanced: pastries, cookies, cereal bars, etc. The latter are, in fact, often packed with sugars and fats: nothing of interest for your body in the long term.

5. It prevents gaining weight

Some claim that skipping breakfast will help you lose weight. Think again!

Many studies have been carried out on the subject and the conclusions are surprising: people who do not eat in the morning on the contrary have much more difficulty in controlling their weight. The study carried out by The American Journal of Epidemiology shows that people who skip breakfast are those who are more affected by overweight or obesity.

These results could be explained, among other things, by the fact that, not having satisfied their morning hunger, these people would be more inclined to snack and consume higher calorie meals or snacks to compensate for their hunger at the next meal.

6. It boosts metabolism

Another benefit of breakfast: did you know that eating a good breakfast in the morning would stimulate the body's metabolism? This first meal of the day signals the body to burn calories, thereby preventing fat storage and massive weight gain.

Another point that would confirm that eating breakfast would stabilize your weight and not gain it!

7. It allows you to eat healthier

Eating a breakfast is one of the attitudes to have in order to have a balanced diet. It allows you to have a structured diet with meals taken at regular times.

It is also an opportunity for us to consume foods that are lacking in our diet: I am thinking in particular of fruits, which we tend to consume in insufficient quantities. Breakfast then becomes an easier opportunity to eat it, and consequently to reach the 5 recommended fruits and vegetables per day.

BENEFITS OF HAVING A HEALTHY AND CORRECT BREAKFAST EVERY MORNING

It is not just a matter of habit; breakfast is one of the main meals, which we should not forget...

Are you used to having breakfast? Or rather, the correct question should be: "Are you sure you can have a healthy and balanced breakfast?"

Maybe, you don't know that the right breakfast has benefits that are carried throughout the day. Here they are

8. You will lose excess weight.

Consistently eating a healthy breakfast can help you lose weight and maintain weight loss. One possible reason is that if you get used to having breakfast, you feel less hungry later in the day, and therefore the chances of having an "incorrect" snack are also reduced.

9. You will be inspired to make healthy choices throughout the day.

A healthy breakfast stimulates in you the desire to make good choices throughout the day. If you grab a quick coffee and have a brioche in the corner of the tea machine in the office, you'll be on a war footing for the rest of the day.

10. Vitamins and minerals mon amour

Skipping breakfast means a missed opportunity to consume your daily requirement of important vitamins and minerals. No need to be a great chef - often a simple, quick, healthy breakfast will provide you with the vitamins and minerals your body needs to function perfectly.

11. You will have more energy.

A nutritious breakfast is a great fuel for your body. Some publications describe that different foods are converted into energy: while some foods give a quick boost of energy, other foods provide the most lasting reserves, ready to be used throughout the day.

12. Heart attack risk decreases

At Harvard, a 2013 study stated that men who skip breakfast regularly had a 27% higher risk of heart attack or death from coronary artery disease than men who they made breakfast. Men who don't eat breakfast are likely to feel hungrier later in the day and eat more food at night, which could be associated with several risk factors for these diseases.

13. You will have a better ability to solve problems.

According to the American Dietetic Association, children who eat breakfast have better concentration, more problem-solving skills and hand-eye coordination. These are good reasons to have a healthy breakfast and make it a priority for the whole family.

14. You will start the day with a better mindset.

Sitting down and enjoying an early breakfast can help start the day fresh up. Eating can decrease your nervous hunger. And by taking your mind off, your mood will thank you.

WHAT TO EAT?

Breakfast

Go back to the beginning of the article. A breakfast consists of a grain product, a piece of fruit, a dairy product and a drink. For lack of time or appetite, breakfast is often overlooked. However, it is essential for a balanced diet. This first meal of the day allows you to regain your strength after a full night without eating.

According to the National Health Nutrition Program (PNNS), an ideal breakfast consists of:

- A cereal product: bread, rusks, breakfast cereals.
- A fruit: apple, banana, apricots, pear ... or 100% pure fruit juice
- A dairy product: milk or yogurt
- A drink: tea or coffee, avoiding sweetening

For some, the lack of appetite when waking up does not encourage eating a hearty breakfast. It is then preferable to wake up gently to start the day well. Some functions are still a little asleep, to wake up and open up your appetite, one of the solutions is to drink a glass of water or a fruit juice upon rising.

Those short on time can opt for a nomadic breakfast with a small packet of cereals or a cereal bar, yogurt and a small bottle of water.

SMOOTHIES AND DRINK RECIPES FOR BREAKFAST

UNICORN SMOOTHIE BOWL

Preparation time 10 minutes

Servings 1

INGREDIENTS

- 2 frozen bananas cut into pieces
- ½ ripe avocados
- 125 ml milk
- 2 tsp of spirulina
- 1 tsp of vanilla powder

For unicorn decoration

- 1 ice cream cone
- 1 banana
- 1 strawberry
- 2 tbsp of granola
- Seeds of your choice

PREPARATION

1. Put all the ingredients in your blender and mix to obtain a homogeneous mass.
2. Pour into a bowl, then decorate as in the photo. Use the seeds.

RASPBERRY SMOOTHIE BOWL

Preparation time 15minutes

Servings 1

INGREDIENTS

Per bowl:

- ❖ 150 g of fresh raspberries
- ❖ 125 ml of yogurt + supplement
- ❖ 5 dates

Presentation:

- ❖ Some raspberries
- ❖ 1-2 tbsp of blueberries
- ❖ 1-2 tbsp blackberries
- ❖ 1 sprig of mint
- ❖ 1 tbsp walnuts and pine nuts
- ❖ 1 tbsp of granola or cruesli

PREPARATION

1. Pit the dates.
2. Mix the raspberries with the yogurt and the dates.
3. Serve in a dish or bowl.

Topping:

1. Top the smoothie with a few raspberries, blueberries and blackberries.
2. Sprinkle with chopped walnuts, pine nuts and granola, and top again with a splash of fresh yogurt.
3. Decorate the whole with a sprig of mint.

RASPBERRY-BLACKBERRY SMOOTHIE

Preparation time 5 minutes

Servings 2

INGREDIENTS

- ❖ 50 g blackberries + a few for garnish
- ❖ 50 g raspberries
- ❖ 180 ml iced coconut water (or milk)
- ❖ 180 ml whole yogurt
- ❖ 1 sachet of vanilla sugar
- ❖ Garnish
- ❖ a few sprigs of basil

PREPARATION

1. In a blender, finely mix all the ingredients except the basil.

2. Pour the smoothie into the glasses

STRAWBERRY-LEMON SMOOTHIE

Preparation time 5minutes

Servings 2

INGREDIENTS

- ❖ 150g fresh strawberries + a few for garnish
- ❖ 1 small handful of coriander leaves
- ❖ 2 tbsp of fresh lemon juice
- ❖ 300 ml of milk
- ❖ 2 tbsp of honey
- ❖ 1 handful of ice cubes

PREPARATION

1. Put all the ingredients in a blender and mix them until you get a creamy smoothie.
2. Fill the glasses with ice cubes.
3. Pour the smoothie into the glasses.
4. Decorate with a strawberry and a sprig of coriander.

BLUEBERRY-CHERRY SMOOTHIE

Preparation time 10 minutes

Servings 2

INGREDIENTS

- ❖ 150g fresh cherries, pitted + a few for garnish
- ❖ 50 g blueberries
- ❖ 250 ml whole yogurt
- ❖ 2 tsp of agave syrup
- ❖ 1 handful of ice cubes
- ❖ Garnish
- ❖ 2 tsp of seeds

PREPARATION

1. Finely mix all the ingredients in a blender.

2. Pour the smoothie into the glasses and decorate with a few seeds and a cherry.

CHERRY-CHOCOLATE SMOOTHIE

Preparation time 15 minutes

Servings

INGREDIENTS

- ❖ 1 cup of cherries
- ❖ 3 tbsp coconut shavings
- ❖ 3 tbsp of cocoa powder
- ❖ 5 tbsp of icing sugar
- ❖ 1 cup of sour cream
- ❖ 600 ml milk

PREPARATION

1. Pit the cherries; pour all the ingredients into a blender.
2. Mix and your smoothie is ready!

JULIA ROSS

RED FRUIT SMOOTHIE WITH YOGURT

Preparation time 15 minutes

Servings 4

INGREDIENTS

- ❖ 200 g of red fruits: strawberries , currants , blueberries , raspberries , blackcurrants , cherries , ...
- ❖ 200 ml whole yogurt
- ❖ 1 tbsp of honey

PREPARATION

1. Wash the fruits and remove all their little tails.
2. Mix all the ingredients in a blender.
3. Pour everything into a glass and stick a straw in it!
4. You can also spice up the smoothie with sugar or syrup.

COTTAGE CHEESE, PLUMS, RED FRUITS AND GINGERBREAD

Preparation time 15

Servings 6

INGREDIENTS

- ❖ 2 plums
- ❖ 250 g strawberries
- ❖ 250 g cherries
- ❖ 50 g sugar
- ❖ 4 slices of Belgian gingerbread
- ❖ 400 g of whole cottage cheese

PREPARATION

1. Clean the plums and stone them. Clean the strawberries and remove their crowns. Clean the cherries remove their stems and stone them.
2. Set a few strawberries, cherries and a few pieces of plums aside for finishing.
3. Put the rest of the fruit in a saucepan and bring to a boil. Leave to cook for about 10 minutes over low heat.
4. Add sugar according to your taste, then let cool.
5. Mix finely and pass through a sieve.
6. Cut the rest of the fruit into pieces.
7. Cut the slices of gingerbread into small cubes.
8. Heat a non-stick pan and toast the diced gingerbread to make them crunchy. Then let them rest on absorbent paper.
9. Divide the fruit coulis between bowls. Add the cottage cheese and finish by placing the pieces of plums, strawberries and cherries, then sprinkle with toasted gingerbread.

SALAD AND FRUIT SMOOTHIE

Preparation time 15minutes

Servings 4

INGREDIENTS

- ❖ 3 small ones Lettuce heart (s)
- ❖ 1 Cucumber (noun)
- ❖ 1 Kiwi (s), with peel
- ❖ 1 Apple, 2 apples depending on size
- ❖ 1 half Galia melon
- ❖ 50 ml Elderflower syrup
- ❖ 500 ml Mineral water
- ❖ 1 tbsp Honey, creamy
- ❖ Ginger or lime

PREPARATION

1. Thoroughly clean the fruit and vegetables and then cut them into pieces.
2. Remove the seeds from the pulp of the melon. I process the kiwi and apple with their skin and core.
3. Put in the blender, add the liquid ingredients and honey and mix everything for about 1 minute.
4. If you want, you can add a little ginger or lime.

FRUIT SMOOTHIE WITH ELDERBERRY SYRUP

Preparation time 5 minutes

Servings 4

INGREDIENTS

- ❖ 2 Kiwi (s)
- ❖ 1 Mango (s), ripe
- ❖ 1 Banana (noun)
- ❖ 50 ml elderberry syrup
- ❖ 200 ml water

PREPARATION

1. Peel the kiwi fruit and, if necessary, cut the stalk out in the middle. Peel the banana and cut or break into slightly smaller pieces. Peel the mango and cut the pulp from the stone. Put everything together in a blender.
2. Put the elderberry syrup and the water in the blender as well. Now let the mixer run at level 2 - 3 for about 1 minute.
3. Ready to serve.

FRUIT-GINGER-COFFEE SMOOTHIE

Preparation time 5 minutes

Servings 4

INGREDIENTS

- ❖ 1 largeOrange (noun)
- ❖ 2 largePear (noun)
- ❖ 3 Kiwi (s)
- ❖ 3 cm Ginger, approx
- ❖ Orange juice to fill up
- ❖ 100 mlStrong coffee or espresso

PREPARATION

1. Peel the orange and cut into medium-sized pieces, quarter the pears, remove the pulp from the kiwi fruit. Put everything together in the blender.
2. Cut off about 3 cm from a finger-thick piece of the ginger root, wash and scrape off the peel with a coffee spoon. This amount of ginger develops a considerable spiciness in the smoothie. Depending on your preferences, you can also use more or less ginger.
3. Put the ginger in the blender as well. If the mixer is not very strong, cut the ginger into small pieces beforehand. Add orange juice as a liquid as desired. I usually take a large glass, around 250 ml. Finally, add the strong coffee and puree everything.
4. The smoothie tastes fruity with a nice, slightly spicy note of ginger and a light coffee aroma.

BERRY SMOOTHIE

Preparation time 10 minutes

Servings 1

INGREDIENTS

- ❖ 40 g Blueberries, (blueberries)
- ❖ 85 g Raspberries
- ❖ 1 teaspoon honey
- ❖ 230 g Natural yoghurt

PREPARATION

1. Put the blueberries in a blender and puree briefly. Add the raspberries, honey and yoghurt and puree them finely. Pour into a glass and serve with breakfast or in between.
2. You can also add a little more honey or sugar if it's not sweet enough. The recipe is for a large jar.

SMOOTHIE BOWL DUO

Preparation time 15 minutes

Servings 1

INGREDIENTS

- ❖ 2 small ones Blood orange (noun)
- ❖ 1 Peach (s)
- ❖ 2 handfuls spinach
- ❖ 1 half Banana (noun)
- ❖ 1 small Piece (s) ginger
- ❖ 1 Lemon (s), juice of it
- ❖ 1 handful Nuts, seeds, desiccated coconut (whatever you like)
- ❖ 2 glasswater

PREPARATION

1. Cut everything into small pieces.
2. Mix the "red" ingredients (blood orange and peach) with a small glass of water and set aside.
3. Then mix the spinach, banana, ginger and lemon juice with water.
4. Pour both smoothies in a bowl or large plate at the same time. Finally, garnish everything with delicious toppings and enjoy!

GREEN VITAMIN BOMB

Preparation time 10 minutes

Cooking / baking time 2 minutes

Servings 1

INGREDIENTS

- ❖ 100 g Lamb's lettuce
- ❖ 8 sheets Lettuce (s)
- ❖ ½ Lemon (organic lemon)
- ❖ 1 Apple
- ❖ 2 Kiwi (s)
- ❖ 800 ml Water, still
- ❖ 1 tbsp Chia seeds
- ❖ 1 tbsp Sugar or xucker

PREPARATION

1. Peel and quarter the kiwi fruit. Wash the apple, remove the stem and flower and cut into quarters. Wash the lemon and cut into pieces with the peel. Wash the salad.
2. Put the fruit first, then the salad in the blender. Add the chia seeds and possibly xucker and pour in the water. Mix for 2 minutes at the highest level or set the program for a green smoothie.
3. Can be kept in the refrigerator for 2 - 3 days

SMOOTHIE BOWL

Preparation time 5 minutes

Servings 1

INGREDIENTS

- ❖ 1 smaller Apple
- ❖ 1 small Orange (noun)
- ❖ 1 handful Fruit, TK
- ❖ Little Soy milk (soy drink) or water
- ❖ oatmeal
- ❖ linseed
- ❖ Dried fruits

PREPARATION

1. First cut the fruit into small pieces and put it in a blender. Then add the frozen fruit and some water or soy milk and mix.
2. Now arrange the smoothie in a bowl and decorate as desired. I like to use oatmeal, flaxseed, and dried fruit.
3. The fruit and the ingredients for decoration can of course be changed according to taste.
4. It's a quick, healthy, tasty breakfast that looks really nice too.

RASPBERRY AND BEAN SMOOTHIE

Preparation 10 minutes

Rest time 20 minutes

Servings 1

INGREDIENTS

- ❖ 20 g Oatmeal, or flake mixture
- ❖ 50 ml Oat milk (oat drink)
- ❖ 50 g Raspberries, frozen goods
- ❖ 100 g Beans, white, cooked, drained
- ❖ 10 g Almond butter, optional
- ❖ 1 m-large Pear (s), or other fruit
- ❖ ½ Banana (noun)

PREPARATION

1. Put the oat flakes with the oat milk or an oat drink in the container of the blender or smoothie maker and let it soak for at least 10 - 20 minutes. With coarse flakes, better longer so that the smoothie will be nice and creamy later. Then add the remaining ingredients, preferably in the order shown.
2. Mix for 30 - 60 seconds; if necessary add some oat drink, water or apple juice, for example, to achieve the desired consistency. The smoothie should not become too thin, it is spooned and intended as a whole meal.
3. Pour into a glass and enjoy.
4. You can use beans that you cooked yourself, or beans from a jar or can. The fruit is variable, but should be ripe so that additional sweetness can be dispensed with. Instead of almond butter, ground vanilla or other spices also taste good. The finished smoothie can be decorated as desired, e.g. B. with fresh mint, finely diced fruit, chocolate sprinkles or chopped nuts.

PUMPKIN, BANANA AND AVOCADO SMOOTHIE BOWL

Preparation time 20 minutes

Servings 1

INGREDIENTS

- ❖ 120 g Hokkaido pumpkin (se)
- ❖ 1 small Banana (noun)
- ❖ ½ Avocado (s)
- ❖ ½ Orange (n), organic
- ❖ 200 g lowfat quark
- ❖ 1 small Disk (noun) ginger
- ❖ 1 Vanilla pod (noun)
- ❖ n. B. Milk or yogurt
- ❖ n. B. Fruit of your choice, e.g. B. berries or apples
- ❖ n. B. Nuts or coconut chips or cocoa nibs

PREPARATION

1. Chop the pumpkin, banana and ginger, rub off the peel of the orange and chop the pulp as well. Place in a mixing bowl with the low-fat quark and avocado.
2. Slit open the side of the vanilla pod and put the scraped out pulp into the container. If you have a strong mixer or hand blender, you can also cut up the pod yourself and add it to the mixture.
3. Mix everything to a homogeneous mass, diluting with yoghurt or milk if necessary.
4. Pour the mixture into a bowl and decorate with fruit, nuts, coconut chips or cocoa nibs to taste.

BANANA-STRAWBERRY SMOOTHIE BOWL

Preparation time 15 minutes

Servings 2

INGREDIENTS

- ❖ 2 Banana (s), sliced and frozen, set aside a few slices for decoration
- ❖ 200 g Set aside strawberries and a few strawberries for decoration
- ❖ 250 g Yogurt, possibly more
- ❖ 3 tsp Cocoa, sweetened

For decoration:

- ❖ Possibly Muesli (crunchy muesli from the database)
- ❖ Possibly Almond sticks
- ❖ Possibly linseed
- ❖ Cereals at will
- ❖ Fruit at will

PREPARATION

1. Put the sliced and frozen banana slices with strawberries, yoghurt and cocoa powder in a blender and puree. If necessary, milk or juice can also be added, but the mixture should be spoonable and not too runny.
2. Then fill the fruit and yogurt puree into bowls and decorate with sliced fruit, muesli, almond sticks and flax seeds. There are no limits to the decoration.
3. Enjoy immediately.
4. Delicious breakfast or snack in summer.

STRAWBERRY JAM WITH VANILLA

Preparation time 20 minutes

Servings 1

INGREDIENTS

- ❖ 1 kg Strawberries, mashed
- ❖ 2 Vanilla pod (s), the pulp of it
- ❖ 1 Lime (noun)
- ❖ 1 bag / n Preserving sugar, 2: 1

PREPARATION

1. Clean, wash and puree the strawberries, put them in a saucepan. Cut the vanilla pods lengthways and scrape out the pulp, add to the strawberry purée. Squeeze the lime and add the juice.
2. Boil 2: 1 with the preserving sugar according to the instructions on the packet.
3. Fill into glasses while still hot and turn them upside down to draw.

KIWI - MANGO - PEPPERMINT JAM

Preparation time 30 minutes

Servings 1

INGREDIENTS

- ❖ 250 g Kiwi (s)
- ❖ 250 g Mango (s), sliced, weighed
- ❖ 2 branch / s peppermint
- ❖ 250 g Preserving sugar (2: 1)

PREPARATION

1. Chop the kiwis and mango and puree. Mix with the preserving sugar and add the peppermint sprigs.
2. Bring to the boil in a saucepan and let it simmer for 4 minutes. Fish out the peppermint and pour the jam into jars that have been rinsed with hot water. Let it steep for five minutes.

YOGURT RECIPES
FOR BREAKFAST

YOGHURT DONUT

Preparation time10 minutes

Cooking 30 minutes

 Servings 4

INGREDIENTS

- ❖ 3 eggs
- ❖ 3 jars of flour
- ❖ 2 jars of sugar
- ❖ 1 jar of natural yogurt of 125 g
- ❖ 1 jar of seed oil
- ❖ 1 sachet of baking powder
- ❖ 2 tablespoons of milk
- ❖ butter
- ❖ powdered sugar

PREPARATION

1. To prepare the yoghurt donut, start by putting eggs, flour, yoghurt, sugar, oil, yeast and milk in the blender, stirring until a homogeneous mixture is obtained.
2. Grease a 24 cm diameter donut mold, sprinkle with icing sugar, pour the mixture and place in a preheated oven at 180 ° to cook for half an hour.
3. Let it cool before unmolding. Serve the yogurt donut after covering it with powdered sugar

RASPBERRY AND YOGURT CREAM

Preparation time 10 minutes

Servings 4

INGREDIENTS

- ❖ 500 g of whole yogurt
- ❖ 130 g of powdered sugar
- ❖ 5 dl of cream
- ❖ 200 g of raspberries
- ❖ small mint leaves
- ❖ a few tablespoons of granulated sugar

PREPARATION

1. Blend the raspberries, except for some which, kept aside, will be used for the final garnish. Whip the cream with the icing sugar, a little at a time; gently add the yogurt and then the raspberry smoothie.
2. Pour the mixture into a large crystal bowl, garnish it with the remaining raspberries and mint leaves sprinkled with slightly moistened granulated sugar.
3. Keep in the fridge until ready to serve.

AVOCADO YOGURT CREAM

Preparation time 25 minutes

Cooking time 10 minutes

Servings 4

INGREDIENTS

- ❖ 250 g of whole white yogurt
- ❖ 100 g of hazelnuts
- ❖ 50 g of honey
- ❖ 1 avocado

PREPARATION

1. In a preheated oven at 170 °, toast the hazelnuts for about ten minutes. Remove the skin by rubbing them with a kitchen towel, then pass them in the food processor.
2. Pour the yogurt into a bowl, add the honey and mix until a thick and homogeneous cream is obtained.
3. Peel the avocado, remove the stone, cut the pulp into regular cubes and add them quickly (otherwise they blacken) to the yogurt cream, mixing gently.
4. Pour the mixture into a glass bowl and sprinkle the surface with the chopped hazelnuts. Keep cool before serving.

YOGURT, CUCUMBER AND MELON CREAM

Preparation time 20 min

Servings 4

INGREDIENTS

- ❖ 200 g of natural cow's milk or soy yogurt
- ❖ 1 cucumber
- ❖ 4 slices of melon
- ❖ 1 lemon
- ❖ 1 spelled piada with olive oil
- ❖ fresh mint
- ❖ extra virgin olive oil
- ❖ salt
- ❖ black pepper

PREPARATION

1. Cut the melon into cubes and season it with salt, a little pepper and oil. We mix, let it flavor and in the meantime we peel and dice the outer part of the cucumber, removing the seeds.
2. In a bowl, mix the yogurt with the juice of one lemon, salt, black pepper, fresh mint and diced cucumber.
3. Blend everything in the mixer adding a few tablespoons of oil to whip the sauce.
4. We place the yogurt and cucumber cream on the bottom of the glasses, complete with the melon and a grind of black pepper and serve with the toasted piada cut into strips.

MUESLI WITH GREEK YOGURT, RASPBERRIES AND PISTACHIOS

Preparation time 20 minutes

Cooking time 10 minutes

Servings 4

INGREDIENTS

- ❖ 700 g of Greek yogurt
- ❖ 2 tablespoons of agave syrup
- ❖ 4 tablespoons of chocolate granola
- ❖ 15 g of chopped pistachios
- ❖ 12 raspberries
- ❖ mint

FOR THE COULIS:

- ❖ 280 g of mixed red fruits (strawberries, blueberries, raspberries)
- ❖ 60 g of brown sugar
- ❖ 2 tablespoons of lemon juice

PREPARATION

1. Wash the fruit and let it dry in a saucepan for two minutes.
2. Add the lemon juice and brown sugar, mix and cook until it begins to thicken.
3. Blend, pass the coulis through a colander, distribute on the bottom of four small glasses and allow to cool.
4. Mix the Greek yogurt well and distribute the first 350 grams in the small glasses to cover the coulis. Add a tablespoon of granola for each serving.
5. Cover with the remaining 350 g of Greek yogurt, if necessary with the help of a pastry bag. Decorated with fresh raspberries, mint and chopped pistachios.
6. Let it rest in the fridge for 20 minutes and serve with agave syrup.

MELON BALLS IN MINT FLAVORED YOGURT

Preparation time 15 minutes

Servings 6

INGREDIENTS

- ❖ 2 melons
- ❖ 3 creamy yogurts
- ❖ 4 teaspoons of honey
- ❖ 2 sprigs of mint

PREPARATION

1. Wash the mint leaves, dry them and cut them up. In a bowl, mix the yogurt with the honey and the chopped mint leaves, then let it rest for two or three hours in the refrigerator.
2. Cut the melons in half, remove seeds and filaments, from the pulp obtained with the digger all possible balls.
3. Mix them with the yogurt sauce and pour the mixture into a large glass bowl. Leave to rest for ten minutes in the refrigerator before serving.

SWEET YOGURT BRAID

Preparation time 35 minutes

Cooking/ baking time 40 minutes

Servings 8

INGREDIENTS

FOR TWO BRAIDS

- ❖ 25 g of brewer's yeast
- ❖ 1/2 dl of milk
- ❖ 1 teaspoon of granulated sugar + one for the surface
- ❖ 650 g of flour 00
- ❖ 2 eggs + 1 yolk at room temperature
- ❖ 150 g of orange blossom honey
- ❖ 250 g of Greek yogurt
- ❖ 60 g of soft butter
- ❖ 30 g of sliced almonds
- ❖ 1 pinch of salt

PREPARATION

1. To make the sweet yogurt braid, prepare yeast by crumbling the brewer's yeast in a bowl and combining half a deciliter of warm milk plus a teaspoon of sugar. Stir with a spoon, or with your fingertips, until the yeast is completely dissolved. Then add 50 grams of sifted flour knead quickly and cover the bowl with cling film. Let it rise in a warm and sheltered place for at least 30 minutes.

2. After this time, break the eggs into the mixer bowl, add the honey, yogurt and a pinch of salt and mix with a whisk for 5 minutes.

3. Add the remaining sifted flour, the prepared baking powder and the diced soft butter to the mixture.

4. Now mount the hook and knead everything for 10 minutes until the dough is smooth and elastic. Cover the bowl with cling film and let the dough rise for 2 hours. In the absence of the planetary

mixer, you can carry out the same operations with an electric whisk, to whip the eggs with the ingredients in step 2, and then knead by hand.

5. Take the dough, deflate it and divide it into two equal parts and then each into three loaves.

6. From each dough, make a loaf and then intertwine them three by three to obtain two braids.

7. Transfer the braids onto a baking sheet lined with baking paper, taking care to fold the ends down and arrange them well spaced so that during the last leavening phase they do not stick together. Then let them rise, covered with a floured cloth, for 30 minutes.

8. Gently brush the two braids with the egg yolk, beaten together with a couple of tablespoons of milk, sprinkle them with the sliced almonds and sugar and bake in a preheated oven at 200 ° for 10 minutes. Then lower the temperature to 180 ° and continue cooking for another 30 minutes. Remove the yogurt braids from the oven, and let them cool on a wire rack before serving.

9. Serve the sweet yogurt braid accompanied by your favorite jam or honey.

YOGURT AND PLUMS

Preparation time 15 minutes

Servings 6

INGREDIENTS

- ❖ 700 g of low-fat yogurt
- ❖ 250 g of pitted dried plums
- ❖ 2 egg whites
- ❖ 2 tablespoons of sugar
- ❖ 6 small meringues
- ❖ 1 centimeter of ginger root
- ❖ 1 tablespoon of kirsch
- ❖ flaked almonds

PREPARATION

1. Aside three prunes for the garnish, blend all the others with the yogurt, sugar, half a teaspoon of grated ginger, the kirsch.
2. Pour the smoothie into a bowl; add the whipped egg whites until stiff peaks.
3. Divide the mousse into six crystal glasses, seal them with cling film, keep them in the refrigerator until ready to serve.
4. Before serving, garnish each glass with a small meringue, half a plum and a few flakes of almonds.

GRANOLA WITH BERRIES AND YOGURT

Preparation time 20 minutes

Cooking time 50 minutes

Rest 10 minutes

Servings 4

INGREDIENTS

- ❖ 500 g of whole yogurt
- ❖ 300 g of rolled oats
- ❖ 120 g of wild strawberries
- ❖ 100 g of blueberries
- ❖ 2 bananas
- ❖ 100 g of unpeeled almonds
- ❖ 100 g of raisins
- ❖ 50 g of acacia honey
- ❖ 50 g of brown sugar
- ❖ 50 g of mixed seeds between sunflower and flax pumpkin
- ❖ peanut oil

PREPARATION

1. In a bowl, mix the oat flakes with the coarsely chopped almonds and the mixed seeds. Pour the honey into a saucepan with the brown sugar and two tablespoons of oil. Heat over low heat until the sugar has dissolved.

2. Pour the syrup into the bowl with the dry ingredients and mix well until the liquid part is absorbed. Spread the crumbled mixture with a spatula on a baking sheet lined with baking paper without pressing too much and cook the granola in a preheated oven at 150 ° for about 30 minutes. Every 10 minutes remove the pan and mix.

3. Soften the raisins in warm water for 10 minutes, drain, dry and mix with the other ingredients, continuing to cook in the oven for another 10 minutes. Let it cool and place the granola in glass jars where it can be stored for a couple of weeks.

4. Pour the yogurt into four bowls, add the bananas cut into chunks and the berries, sprinkle everything with plenty of granola and serve.

MUFFIN WITH YOGURT

Preparation time10 minutes

Cooking/ Baking time 25 minutes

Servings 6

INGREDIENTS

- ❖ 300 g of self-raising flour
- ❖ 150 g of butter
- ❖ 60 g of sugar
- ❖ 2 dl of milk
- ❖ 180 ml of whole yogurt
- ❖ 2 eggs
- ❖ 1 untreated lemon
- ❖ 1 teaspoon of vanilla baking powder
- ❖ salt

PREPARATION

1. Melt the butter over a very low heat and let it cool. Sift the flour with the baking powder and drop it directly into a bowl. Add the grated lemon zest, sugar and a pinch of salt.
2. Break the eggs into a second bowl, beat them with a fork, add the milk, yogurt and finally the melted butter. Pour the mixture into the bowl with the flour and mix until the ingredients are blended, without working the mixture too much.
3. Divide the mixture into cups arranged in 12 muffin molds and bake the sweets in the central part of the oven at 180 degrees for 25 minutes. Let them rest for 5 minutes and transfer them to a wire rack.
4. When the muffins have cooled, arrange them on a serving dish and sprinkle with icing sugar. These simple and quick sweets of Anglo-Saxon origin are perfect for a delicious breakfast, a snack or a tea with friends.

GRANOLA RECIPES
FOR BREAKFAST

HOMEMADE GRANOLA

Preparation time 10 minutes

Cooking time 40 minutes

Servings 6

INGREDIENTS

- ❖ 700 g of rolled oats
- ❖ 70 g of almonds
- ❖ 70 g of hazelnuts
- ❖ 70 g of cashews
- ❖ 100 g of dehydrated red fruits and raisins
- ❖ 130 g of maple syrup
- ❖ 130 g of honey
- ❖ vegetable oil
- ❖ half a glass of water

PREPARATION

1. Arrange the oat flakes, almonds, hazelnuts, cashews, dehydrated red fruits and raisins in a bowl. Sprinkle them with maple syrup, oil, honey and half a glass of water, then mix carefully.

2. Spread the preparation on a large baking sheet lined with parchment paper. For optimum yield, make sure the ingredients are well leveled and not too overlapping. Bake for an hour in a preheated oven at 160 °. After about 20 minutes of cooking, turn the granola with a spoon, without crumbling it, to obtain an even cooking. Continue cooking until the granola is crunchy. Let it cool and finally break it with your hands.

3. Eat the granola immediately with yogurt and fresh fruit or store it in hermetically sealed jars for up to a week.

GRANOLA WITH DRIED FRUITS

Preparation time 10 minutes

Cooking / Baking time 30 minutes

Servings 10

- ❖ pistachios50 g
- ❖ dried apricots50 g
- ❖ mango (dried)50 g
- ❖ barley (flaked)250 g
- ❖ pumpkin seeds40 g
- ❖ Sesame seeds1 tbsp
- ❖ agave syrup3 tbsp
- ❖ sunflower oil3 tbsp
- ❖ orange (zest)1

PREPARATION

1. Preheat the oven to 180 ° C. Chop the pistachios, apricots and mango roughly. Place all the ingredients, except the dried fruit, in a bowl.
2. Heat the agave syrup and oil and throw in the dry ingredients. Add the thunderstorm zest and mix everything.
3. Spread everything out on a baking sheet lined with baking paper and bake for 20 minutes. Stir regularly. Let cool completely and then add the dried fruit.

SWEET GRANOLA WITH APPLESAUCE

Preparation time 10 minutes

Cooking / Baking time 40 minutes

Servings 15

INGREDIENTS

- ❖ pecan nuts40 g
- ❖ flaked almonds40 g
- ❖ Hazelnut40 g
- ❖ oatmeal300 g
- ❖ coconut shavings40 g
- ❖ pumpkin seeds4 tbsp
- ❖ raspberries (dried)40 g
- ❖ cinnamon½ tsp
- ❖ cumin¼ tsp
- ❖ applesauce150 g
- ❖ honey2 tbsp

PREPARATION

1. Preheat the oven to 180 ° C. Coarsely chop the nuts. Combine all the ingredients except the raspberries.
2. Spread the mixture evenly on a baking sheet lined with baking paper and bake for 30 min. Stir regularly.
3. Let cool completely and add the dried raspberries.

PEANUT BUTTER AND CHOCOLATE GRANOLA

Preparation time 10 minutes

Cooking / baking time30 minutes

Servings 15

INGREDIENTS

- ❖ peanuts40 g
- ❖ pecan nuts40 g
- ❖ Peanut butter80 g
- ❖ honey3 tbsp
- ❖ coconut oil4 tbsp
- ❖ vanilla extract½ tsp
- ❖ barley (flaked)250 g
- ❖ bananas (dried)50 g
- ❖ chocolate chips50 g

PREPARATION

1. Preheat the oven to 180 ° C. Coarsely chop the peanuts and walnuts. Melt the peanut butter, honey, coconut oil and vanilla extract over low heat.
2. Stir in the barley flakes, peanuts and walnuts. Spread everything out on a baking sheet lined with parchment paper. Bake for 20 min.
3. Let cool and finally add the dried bananas and chocolate chips.

HOMEMADE CHOCOLATE GRANOLA

Preparation time 10 minutes

Cooking time 35 minutes

Servings 1

INGREDIENTS

- ❖ hazelnuts (blanched)150 g
- ❖ oatmeal250 g
- ❖ oil (coconut)2 tbsp
- ❖ acacia honey (or agave syrup)2 tbsp
- ❖ water6 tbsp
- ❖ dark chocolate (70% cocoa, in lozenges)50 g

PREPARATION

1. Preheat the oven to 160 ° C. Reduce 100 g of hazelnuts to powder in a food processor: the consistency should resemble flour (no more, otherwise it is a paste of hazelnuts).
2. Pour the oatmeal in a bowl and add the hazelnut flour and the rest of the hazelnuts.
3. Melt the coconut oil and add it to the mixture with the honey and water. Mix. Pour on a baking sheet and cook for 15 to 20 minutes in a hot oven. Stir gently and continue cooking until the cruesli is golden. Let cool and add the chocolate.
4. Good idea: serve the cruesli with blueberries and plain yogurt for example.

ALMOND AND PISTACHIO GRANOLA

Preparation time 10 minutes

Cooking time 30 minutes

Servings 1

INGREDIENTS

- ❖ mixed flakes (oats, barley, spelled, wheat, buckwheat, ...)300 g
- ❖ puffed rice (unsweetened)100 g
- ❖ almonds (chopped)70 g
- ❖ unsalted pistachios70 g
- ❖ pumpkin seeds50 g
- ❖ liquid honey6 tbsp
- ❖ Colza oil3 tbsp
- ❖ gingerbread spices1 tsp
- ❖ liquid vanilla extract1 tbsp
- ❖ dark chocolate (in large pieces)60 g

PREPARATION

1. Pour all the ingredients (except the chocolate) into a bowl and mix vigorously. Leave to stand for 10 minutes to soak the flakes.
2. Spread a sheet of baking paper on a baking sheet and spread the dough there. Place in a non-preheated oven at 150 ° C, stirring every 5 minutes with a fork. Allow about 20 minutes of cooking. Add 10 minutes more if you like very golden and very crispy granola. Let cool on the baking sheet.
3. Break the pieces that are too big with a fork then add the chocolate. Pour into a large airtight jar and store at room temperature. Serve with yogurt, milk, compote... or snack as is.

CRANBERRY GRANOLA

Preparation time 10 minutes

Cooking time 30 minutes

Servings 4

INGREDIENTS

- ❖ oatmeal500 g
- ❖ applesauce250 g
- ❖ cashew nut100 g
- ❖ Hazelnut100 g
- ❖ pistachios100 g
- ❖ pumpkin seeds100 g
- ❖ nuts (chopped)50 g
- ❖ Sun-flower seeds50 g
- ❖ flaked almonds50 g
- ❖ raisins100 g
- ❖ cranberries (dried)100 g
- ❖ honey4 tbsp
- ❖ brown sugar2 tbsp
- ❖ cinnamon powder2 tsp
- ❖ ginger powder1 tsp
- ❖ vanilla sugar2 sachets
- ❖ corn oil4 tbsp

PREPARATION

1. Preheat the oven to 180 ° C. Combine the oatmeal, cashews, hazelnuts, pistachios, squash seeds, walnuts, sunflower seeds and slivered almonds.
2. Heat the applesauce with the honey, brown sugar, cinnamon, ginger and vanilla sugar. Pour this mixture and the oil over the dry mixture. Mix well. Arrange on 2 baking sheets lined with paper.
3. Cook for 25 minutes, stirring regularly so that the granola is colored evenly.

4. Pour the preparation into a dish. Stir in the grapes and cranberries. Let cool then store in jars or small sachets.

SWEET BANANA GRANOLA

Preparation time 10 minutes

Cooking time / Baking time 30 minutes

Servings 10

INGREDIENTS

- ❖ almonds80 g
- ❖ coconut oil2 tbsp
- ❖ honey4 tbsp
- ❖ vanilla1 clove
- ❖ bananas2
- ❖ oatmeal250 g
- ❖ quinoa (flaked)4 tbsp
- ❖ pumpkin seeds50 g
- ❖ ginger powder1 tbsp

PREPARATION

1. Preheat the oven to 180 ° C and line an oven tray with baking paper. Roughly chop the almonds.
2. Melt the coconut oil and honey over low heat. Split the vanilla bean in half lengthwise and scrape the beans with a knife. Add them to the coconut oil as well as the mashed bananas. Mix everything.
3. Pour this mixture over the dry ingredients, stir well and pour onto the baking sheet. Bake for 20 min. stir the granola regularly.

QUINOA AND CRANBERRY GRANOLA

Preparation time 10 minutes

Cooking time 30 minutes

Servings 12

INGREDIENTS

- ❖ nuts30 g
- ❖ quinoa100 g
- ❖ buckwheat (flaked)70 g
- ❖ oatmeal70 g
- ❖ Sun-flower seeds40 g
- ❖ raisins40 g
- ❖ dried cranberries40 g
- ❖ coconut oil3 tbsp
- ❖ agave syrup4 tbsp
- ❖ speculoos spices½ tsp

PREPARATION

1. Preheat the oven to 180 ° C. Line a baking sheet with parchment paper. Coarsely chop the nuts. Place the quinoa, buckwheat and oat flakes, as well as nuts and sunflower seeds in a bowl. Reserve the grapes and cranberries.
2. Melt the coconut oil and agave syrup. Add the speculoos spices and stir well. Pour over the dry ingredients and mix well.
3. Spread everything on the baking sheet and bake for 20 min. Stir regularly. Let the granola cool completely and stir in the raisins and cranberrie

HEALTHY GRANOLA

Preparation time 10 minutes

Cooking time 30 minutes

Servings 6

INGREDIENTS

- ❖ oatmeal1 kg
- ❖ cashew nut100 g
- ❖ Hazelnut100 g
- ❖ pistachios100 g
- ❖ pumpkin seeds100 g
- ❖ Sun-flower seeds50 g
- ❖ linseed2 tbsp
- ❖ Sesame seeds2 tbsp
- ❖ chia seeds2 tbsp
- ❖ applesauce400 g
- ❖ honey4 tbsp
- ❖ cinnamon1 tsp
- ❖ ginger powder1 tsp
- ❖ vanilla sugar2 sachets
- ❖ raisins100 g
- ❖ cranberries (dried)100 g
- ❖ Goji berries4 tbsp

PREPARATION

1. Preheat the oven to 180 ° C. In a large bowl, mix the oatmeal with the cashews, hazelnuts, pistachios, pumpkin seeds, sunflower seeds, flax seeds, sesame and chia.

2. Heat the compote in a pan with the honey, cinnamon, ground ginger and vanilla sugar. Mix and pour the mixture into the bowl. Mix thoroughly and spread the whole in an even layer on two baking sheets lined with parchment paper.

3. Bake for 20 minutes in a hot oven, the time to lightly color the elements. Pour them into a large salad bowl with the raisins, cranberries and goji berries. Let cool, mix and divide into glass jars.

GRANOLA

Preparation time 15 minutes

Cooking Baking time 45 minutes

Servings 4

INGREDIENTS

- ❖ oatmeal300 g
- ❖ oilseeds (hazelnuts, almonds, cashew or sesame, sunflower, squash)150 g
- ❖ Apple juice12 cl
- ❖ olive oil1 tbsp
- ❖ dried fruits

PREPARATION

1. In a salad bowl, mix the oatmeal and oilseeds (hazelnuts + almonds + cashew or sesame + sunflower + squash), apple juice and olive oil.
2. Spread the mixture out on a baking sheet and bake for 30 minutes at 150 ° C, stirring occasionally.
3. Let cool. Add dried fruits at will, depending on what you have on hand: cranberries, raisins, diced apricots or figs, etc.

OATS RECIPES
FOR BREAKFAST

OATMEAL BREAKFAST WITH STRAWBERRIES

Preparation time 5 minutes

Servings 1

INGREDIENTS

- ❖ oatmeal
- ❖ 6 tablespoons / 45 g
- ❖ Flaxseed (crushed)
- ❖ 2 tablespoons / 15 g
- ❖ Natural oat milk
- ❖ 200 milliliters
- ❖ Strawberries
- ❖ 150 grams

PREPARATION

1. Mix oat flakes, linseed and oat milk in a bowl and let soak for at least 10 minutes, if you like longer or overnight, then it tastes even better.
2. Carefully wash the strawberries, remove the green, cut into small pieces and add to the oatmeal porridge.

CREAM CHEESE OATMEAL BREAKFAST

Preparation time 10 minutes

Servings 1

INGREDIENTS

- ❖ Grained cream cheese
- ❖ 200 grams
- ❖ oatmeal
- ❖ 3 tablespoons / 25 g
- ❖ water
- ❖ 100 milliliters
- ❖ Sour cherry / n
- ❖ 30 grams

PREPARATION

1. Mix the oat flakes with the water and leave to swell for 5 minutes.

2. In the meantime, wash, core and cut the cherries into small pieces and stir the cherry pieces together with the grainy cream cheese into the oat flakes.

OVERNIGT-OATS WITH RASPBERRIES & ALMOND BUTTER

Preparation time 30 minutes

Servings 1

INGREDIENTS

- ❖ Oat flakes (gluten free)
- ❖ 4 tablespoons / 45 g
- ❖ Raspberries (frozen)
- ❖ 4 tablespoons / 60 g
- ❖ Quinoa (puffed)
- ❖ 2 tablespoons / 15 g
- ❖ Greek yogurt
- ❖ 4 tablespoons / 60 g
- ❖ Almond butter
- ❖ 2 tablespoons / 20 g
- ❖ honey
- ❖ 2 teaspoons / 12 g
- ❖ Almond milk
- ❖ 80 grams

PREPARATION

1. For the overnight oats breakfast, mix the oat flakes, half of the raspberries, quinoa pops, yoghurt, almond butter, 1 teaspoon honey and almond milk in a glass and stir well.
2. Place in the refrigerator overnight so that the oatmeal can swell well. Stir briefly the next morning. Tip: If you have to go very quickly: If necessary, 20 minutes of soaking time is enough.
3. Put the rest of the raspberries in a bowl and thaw, mix with 1 teaspoon honey and stir until a liquid sauce is formed. Pour onto the glass with the overnight oats and enjoy.

OAT BRAN BREAD WITHOUT YEAST

Preparation time 5 minutes

Cooking / Baking time 50 minutes

Servings 12

INGREDIENTS

- ❖ 12thpeople
- ❖ Oat bran
- ❖ 280 grams
- ❖ linseed
- ❖ 5 tablespoons / 40 g
- ❖ Low-fat quark (organic)
- ❖ 500 grams
- ❖ Eggs
- ❖ 6 pieces / 350 g
- ❖ baking powder
- ❖ 1 pack / 17 g
- ❖ salt
- ❖ 1 teaspoon / 6 g

PREPARATION

1. Mix oat bran, flaxseed, low-fat quark, eggs and salt and baking powder in a bowl with a mixer or whisk.
2. If you like and tolerate it, you can add other bread spices (caraway, anise, fennel, coriander).
3. Pour the bread dough into a greased loaf tin, score lengthways at the top and bake at 200 ° C fan oven / 220 ° C electric stove for about 50 minutes.
4. Let cool down and enjoy. You can cut about 30 thin slices from a loaf pan. 3 slices count as one serving.
5. You can also bake the oat bran bread as a smaller, flatter bread. To do this, simply halve all the ingredients and also the baking time.

FRUCTOSE-FREE OAT AND COCONUT MUESLI

Preparation time 20 minutes

Servings 2

INGREDIENTS

- ❖ oatmeal
- ❖ 100 gram
- ❖ Almond / n
- ❖ 40 grams
- ❖ Rice syrup
- ❖ 1 tablespoon / 8 g
- ❖ cinnamon
- ❖ ½ teaspoon / 1 g
- ❖ Natural yoghurt
- ❖ 400 grams
- ❖ Coconut flakes
- ❖ 1 tablespoon / 5 g
- ❖ Chia seeds
- ❖ 1 tablespoon / 8 g
- ❖ water
- ❖ 3 tablespoons / 30 g

PREPARATION

1. Mix the chia seeds with 3 tablespoons of water in a small bowl and let soak for 5 minutes.
2. Meanwhile, coarsely chop the almonds and mix with the maple syrup and cinnamon in a cereal bowl.
3. Add the yogurt and oatmeal and mix everything well. Stir in chia seeds.
4. Sprinkle the finished fructose-free oat-nut muesli with coconut flakes. Garnish with other nuts.

GRAIN RECIPES
FOR BREAKFAST

COCOA AND ORANGE BREAD

Preparation time 30 minutes

Waiting time 2 hours

Cooking / Baking time 45 minutes

Servings 1

INGREDIENTS

- ❖ 250 ml milk (1.5% fat)
- ❖ 1 cube of yeast (fresh)
- ❖ 3 tbsp orange blossom honey
- ❖ 1 orange (organic)
- ❖ 300 g spelled flour
- ❖ 80 g corn grits
- ❖ 100 g almonds (ground, roasted)
- ❖ 10 g of salt
- ❖ 50 g cocoa powder
- ❖ Flour (for working)

PREPARATION

1. For cocoa and orange bread, warm the milk to lukewarm. Crumble the yeast in half of the milk. Dissolve these with the honey in the milk and let stand until bubbles appear.
2. Wash the orange with hot water, rub dry, grate the peel finely and fillet the orange, collecting the juice. Cut the fillets into small pieces. Add 2 tablespoons of the orange juice to the rest of the milk.
3. Put the spelled flour, corn grits, almonds, salt, cocoa powder, orange peel and fillets in a mixing bowl. Finally, pour in the yeast-milk mixture. While kneading with the dough hook on the low level with the food processor, gradually add enough of the remaining milk until a light, homogeneous dough is formed.
4. Knead the dough on the floured work surface for about 5 minutes with the balls of your hands, repeatedly beating it up and turning it until it is no longer sticky and elastic, then cover it in a bowl for about 2 hours until its volume has doubled.

5. Cover a baking sheet with parchment paper, place the dough on it as a ball with the dough top facing down and cut crosswise. Cover the dough and let it rest for about 1 hour until the volume has doubled.

6. Preheat the oven to 220 ° C (convection not suitable). Brush the surface of the bread with water and bake the bread on the second rack from the bottom for 40-45 minutes. Take the finished cocoa and orange bread out of the oven and let it cool down completely on a wire rack.

CRUNCHY CEREAL

Preparation time 30 minutes

Cooking / Baking time 30 minutes

Servings 1

INGREDIENTS

- ❖ 3 tbsp coconut oil (Ceres)
- ❖ 250 g oatmeal
- ❖ 80 g nuts (cashews and hazelnuts mixed, whole)
- ❖ 80 g pumpkin seeds
- ❖ 1 pinch of salt
- ❖ some cinnamon (ground)
- ❖ 3 tbsp maple syrup
- ❖ Raisins (to taste)

PREPARATION

1. For the crunchy muesli, first preheat the oven to 180 ° C. Melt the coconut oil.
2. In a large enough bowl, mix the oatmeal, nuts, pumpkin seeds, salt and cinnamon together. Add maple syrup and coconut oil and mix everything well.
3. Spread the mixture evenly on a baking sheet lined with baking paper. Bake for 10 minutes, then turn and bake for another 5-10 minutes. Check again and again so that the muesli doesn't get too dark.
4. The crunchy remove it from the oven let cool and mix with the raisins.

OWL PORRIDGE

Preparation time 15 minutes

Cooking / Baking time 10 minutes

Servings 1

INGREDIENTS

- ❖ 1/2 kiwi
- ❖ 1/2 banana
- ❖ 1/2 orange
- ❖ 1 grapes (dark)
- ❖ 1/2 apple
- ❖ 6 almonds (unpeeled)

For the porridge:

- ❖ 350 ml milk (or water or mixed)
- ❖ 50 g of oatmeal
- ❖ 1-2 tbsp oat bran (optional)
- ❖ 1 pinch of salt

PREPARATION

1. For the owl porridge, first bring all the ingredients for the oatmeal to the boil and simmer for 5-10 minutes, stirring, until the desired consistency is reached.
2. In the meantime, peel the fruit (kiwi, banana and orange). Cut the kiwi and banana into slices. Halve 3-4 banana slices. Cut off the corners of the orange fillets for the feet and beak. Wash grapes and apples. Halve the grape. Core the apple and cut into wedges.
3. Pour the finished porridge into a bowl. For the eyes, place 2 kiwi slices and a banana slice and half a grape on top. Place 3 almonds on top. Put an orange corner as a beak between the eyes. Indicate the feathers below with the halved banana slices. Place an apple slice on the right and left of it for the wings. Place 2 orange corners for the feet under the wings.
4. Serve the owl porridge warm.

SAVORY POWER MUFFINS

Preparation time 30 minutes

Cooking / Baking time 20 minutes

Servings 12

INGREDIENTS

- ❖ 1 einkorn spelled bread
- ❖ 6 eggs
- ❖ 8 slice (s) of cheese (approx. 100 g)
- ❖ 8 slices of ham (approx. 80 g)
- ❖ 1 bell pepper (red)
- ❖ 1 pinch of salt
- ❖ 1 bunch of chives (for decorating)

PREPARATION

1. For spicy power muffins, first cut the einkorn spelled bread into slices and cut out the base for the muffins with a glass.
2. Dice the cheese, ham and paprika and mix with the eggs and a pinch of salt in a bowl.
3. Preheat the oven to 180 ° C hot air.
4. Press the bread circle into the muffin molds and fill up with the mixed mixture.
5. Bake spicy power muffins for 20 minutes at 180 ° C. Serve sprinkled with chopped chives.

YOGURT AND HONEY CREAM WITH CRUNCHY MUESLI AND MELON

Preparation time 15 minutes

Servings 4

INGREDIENTS

- ❖ 600 g yogurt (Greek)
- ❖ 4 tbsp cream cheese
- ❖ 12 tbsp honey
- ❖ 200 g whipped cream
- ❖ 1 packet of crispy muesli
- ❖ 1 chaentais melon
- ❖ 1 Galia melon

PREPARATION

1. For the yoghurt honey cream with crunchy muesli and melon, mix the yoghurt with cream cheese and honey well. Whip up the top and fold in. Pour 2 tablespoons of granola per glass and spread the cream on top.

2. Then spread another 2 tablespoons of muesli on the cream.

3. Cut small, flat triangles from the Charentais melon and cut small, flat tridents from the Gala melon. Put these together into mini carrots (if necessary fix with a toothpick) and place as a garnish on the yoghurt honey cream with crunchy muesli and melon.

EGGS RECIPES
FOR BREAKFAST

BREAKFAST BASIL PIZZA

Preparation time 15 minutes

Cooking / Baking time 15 minutes

Servings 2-3

INGREDIENTS

- ❖ 1 pizza crust (homemade or store-bought)
- ❖ 1/4 cup tubed basil (herbs)
- ❖ 1 cup melted cheese (mozzarella, cheddar, or pizza mix for gratins)
- ❖ 4 small tomatoes, cut in 2 or 4
- ❖ 3 eggs
- ❖ 1 green onion, thinly sliced
- ❖ Fresh basil leaves
- ❖ Salt pepper
- ❖ 1 egg yolk
- ❖ 1 C. Tea water
- ❖ 1/2 lemon
- ❖ 1/2 cup butter

PREPARATION

1. Preheat the oven to 450 ° F.
2. Spread pizza dough if necessary, then set aside on a baking sheet.
3. Prepare the Hollandaise Sauce: Melt the butter in a microwave-safe mug, about 20 to 30 seconds.
4. In a tall, narrow container (such as a 500 ml wide-mouthed Mason jar), place the egg yolk and water. Squeeze the lemon directly into the mixture.
5. With a stand mixer, lather the egg yolk mixture directly into the container, for about 1 minute.
6. Add the still hot butter, a little at a time, continuing to mix. The sauce will swell and become very creamy.
7. On the pizza crust, spread the tube basil.
8. Using a spoon, place hollandaise sauce all over the pizza. Save some for serving.
9. Add the tomatoes and cheese, leaving some space in the middle to break the eggs.

10. Crack the eggs in the center of the pizza. Season well with salt and pepper.

11. Gently grab the baking sheet and place it in the oven. Bake, about 12 to 14 minutes, until the cheese is well melted and the eggs are almost cooked (to taste).

12. Get out of the oven. Add some remaining hollandaise sauce. Garnish with the green onion and a few fresh basil leaves. Enjoy immediately!

HARD-BOILED EGGS

Preparation time 2 minutes

Cooking time 10 minutes

Servings 1

INGREDIENTS

❖ Water

❖ 2 eggs

PREPARATION

1. Place the cold eggs in a saucepan. Cover with at least 1 inch (2.5 cm) of cold water.
2. Cover the pot and quickly bring the water to a boil over high heat. Immediately remove from heat to stop boiling. Let the eggs rest, covered, for 12 minutes.
3. Drain and immediately rinse under cold running water or leave the eggs in the pan until cool.

SPICY AVOCADO EGGS ON TOAST

Preparation time 5 minutes

Cooking time 5 minutes

Servings 4

INGREDIENTS

- ❖ 1 C. at table (15 ml) butter
- ❖ 6 eggs
- ❖ 1/4 tsp tea (1.25 ml) each of salt and pepper
- ❖ 1 ripe avocado, coarsely crushed
- ❖ 2 tbsp at table (30 ml) chopped cilantro
- ❖ 4 slices of rye bread, toasted
- ❖ 2 tbsp tea (10 ml) chili oil

PREPARATION

1. Heat the butter in a large non-stick skillet over medium heat. Using a whisk, combine the eggs, salt and pepper; pour into the pan. Cook, stirring, 2 to 3 minutes or until tender lumps form

2. Remove from heat and gently fold in the avocado and cilantro. Place on the toast and garnish with a drizzle of chili oil.

CLOUD EGGS

Preparation time 15 minutes

Cooking time 10 minutes

Servings 4

INGREDIENTS

- ❖ 4 eggs
- ❖ 1 pinch of salt
- ❖ 1/4 cup (60 ml) grated parmesan
- ❖ 2 bacon slices, cooked and crumbled
- ❖ 1 C. at table (15 ml) fresh chives, finely chopped

PREPARATION

1. Preheat the oven to 425 ° F (220 ° C). Separate the eggs by placing the whites in a large bowl and each of the yolks in a ramekin or small bowl.
2. Using an electric mixer, beat the egg whites and salt until stiff peaks form. Stir in cheese, bacon and chives. Using a spoon, drop the mixture into 4 mounds on a baking sheet lined with parchment paper. Form a deep hollow in the center of each mound.
3. Bake for about 6 to 8 minutes or until the mixture is set and golden brown. Place an egg yolk in the hollow of each mound. Cook for 3 to 5 minutes or until the yolks are the desired doneness.

PEPPER EGGS

Preparation time 10 minutes

Cooking time 7 minutes

Servings 4

INGREDIENTS

- ❖ 1 large bell pepper, red, green or yellow
- ❖ 1 C. tea (5 ml) canola oil
- ❖ 4 eggs
- ❖ 1/4 tsp. tea (1.25 ml) salt
- ❖ 1/4 tsp. tea (1.25 ml) pepper
- ❖ 4 whole grain bread slices
- ❖ 4 tbsp. tea (20 ml) buttery, softened
- ❖ 1/4 cup (60 ml) salsa

PREPARATION

1. Cut off the top and bottom of the pepper, set aside. Cut into 4 1/2-inch rounds; keep the rest of the pepper for later use. Heat oil in a large nonstick skillet over medium-high heat. Add the pepper rings and crack 1 egg in the center of each ring. Season with salt and pepper. Cook, covered, 5 to 7 minutes or until top of yolk is cooked through.
2. Meanwhile, toast bread until golden brown and brush with butter. Cut each slice into 5 soldiers. Serve the eggs with the grilled soldiers and salsa.

PROTEIN RECIPES
FOR BREAKFAST

LUNCH IN A CUP

Preparation time 5 minutes

Cooking time 2 minutes

Servings 1

INGREDIENTS

- ❖ 1 slice of whole grain bread, cubed
- ❖ 2 tbsp. at table (30 ml) seeded and diced tomato
- ❖ 2 tbsp. at table (30 ml) grated cheddar cheese
- ❖ 1 C. at table (15 ml) finely chopped green onion
- ❖ 1 beaten egg
- ❖ 2 tbsp. at table (30 ml) of milk

PREPARATION

1. Mix the bread with the tomato, cheese and green onion. Transfer to a microwave-safe mug. Beat the egg and the milk, then pour over the filling.

2. Microwave on high power (100%) for 60 seconds; let stand 10 seconds. Microwave on high (100%) for 60 seconds longer or until mixture is set.

BOWL OF CREAMY PUMPKIN SPICE OATMEAL

Preparation time 10 minutes

Cooking time 10 minutes

Servings 4

INGREDIENTS

- ❖ 3 eggs
- ❖ 2 1/2 cups (625 ml)   of milk
- ❖ 1 cup (250 ml) quick oatmeal
- ❖ 2 tbsp. at table (30 ml) maple syrup
- ❖ 1 C. at table (15 ml) molasses
- ❖ 1 C. at table (15 ml) pumpkin pie spice
- ❖ 1 C. tea (5 ml) vanilla extract
- ❖ 1 pinch of salt
- ❖ 1/2 cup (125 ml) pure pumpkin puree
- ❖ 1/2 cup (125 ml) plain Greek yogurt
- ❖ 1/3 cup (75 ml) chopped toasted pecans

PREPARATION

1. In a bowl, beat the eggs. Stir in milk, oats, maple syrup, molasses, pumpkin pie spice, vanilla and salt until combined. Transfer the mixture to a saucepan over medium-low heat. Cook, stirring often, for 8 to 10 minutes.

2. Stir in the pumpkin puree and cook for about 2 minutes or until the oatmeal is tender and creamy and the puree is heated through. Divide among 4 bowls. Cover evenly with yogurt and chopped pecans.

TURKEY BACON EGG BREAKFAST CASSEROLE

Preparation time 15 minutes

Cooking / Baking time 35 minutes

Servings 4

INGREDIENTS

- ❖ 4 slices of crustless bread, cut into quarters
- ❖ 6 eggs
- ❖ 1 1/2 cup (375 ml) milk (1%)
- ❖ 4 slices of cooked turkey bacon, diced
- ❖ 1/2 cup (125 ml) light cheddar, grated, divided
- ❖ 1/2 cup (125 ml) sliced mushrooms
- ❖ 1/2 cup (125 ml) frozen hash browns, thawed

PREPARATION

1. Preheat the oven to 350 ° F (180 ° C).
2. Spray 9-inch (23 cm) pan with cooking spray. Place the slices of bread in the pan so that they overlap slightly.
3. Whisk eggs, milk, bacon and 1/4 cup (50 mL) cheese in a large bowl. Add the mushrooms. Pour the mixture over the slices of bread. Sprinkle the potatoes and remaining cheese over the egg mixture.
4. Bake in preheated 350 ° F (180 ° C) oven until lightly browned and knife inserted in center comes out clean, about 35 minutes.

KALE AND EGG WRAP SANDWICH

Preparation time 10 minutes

Cooking / Baking time 12 minutes

Servings 4

INGREDIENTS

- ❖ 8 eggs
- ❖ 1/2 tsp. tea (2.5 ml)   salt
- ❖ 1/4 tsp. tea (1.25 ml) freshly ground pepper
- ❖ 2 tbsp. at table (30 ml) olive oil
- ❖ 2 garlic cloves, minced
- ❖ 1 pinch of hot pepper flakes
- ❖ 2 cups (500 ml) kale, stem removed and finely chopped, lightly packed
- ❖ 4 large whole wheat tortillas (10 in / 25 cm), warmed
- ❖ 1/4 cup (60 ml) hummus
- ❖ 1 tomato, sliced

PREPARATION

1. Beat the eggs with the salt and pepper. In a nonstick skillet, heat oil over medium heat; cook garlic and hot pepper flakes until flavored, about 1 minute. Add the kale; cook until starting to soften, about 2 or 3 minutes.
2. Reduce the heat to medium-low; pour in the egg mixture. Cook, stirring constantly, until eggs are creamy and lightly set, 5 to 8 minutes.
3. Place the tortillas on a work surface. Spread hummus along the center of each tortilla, leaving a gap near the ends. Top with tomatoes and scrambled egg mixture. Fold the bottom of each tortilla over the filling, then fold up the sides and roll up tightly.

EARLY MORNING EGG SANDWICH

Preparation time 5 minutes

Cooking / Baking time 5 minutes

Servings 4

INGREDIENTS

- ❖ 3 tbsp. at table (45 ml) light mayonnaise or salad dressing
- ❖ 2 tbsp. at table (30 ml) milk (1%)
- ❖ 1 C. at table (15 ml) grated parmesan
- ❖ 1 C. tea (5 ml) lemon juice
- ❖ 1/2 tsp. tea (2.5 ml) lemon zest
- ❖ 4 eggs
- ❖ 1 medium tomato, thinly sliced
- ❖ 4 slices of multrigrain, French or Italian bread

PREPARATION

1. In a small microwave-safe bowl, put the mayonnaise and whisk it with the milk. Microwave over medium heat, until heated through, about 45 seconds. Stir after 30 seconds of cooking. Then whisk with the Parmesan, lemon juice and zest until completely combined. Set the sauce aside.
2. Spray a nonstick skillet with cooking spray. Heat the pan over medium heat. Break the eggs into the pan. Poke the yolk out of the eggs with a spatula. Cook the eggs until the desired doneness.
3. Place the tomato slices on 2 slices of bread. Top with the fried eggs. Pour in about 1 tsp. at t. (15 mL) hot sauce on each egg. Cover with remaining slices of bread.

SANDWICH AND TOAST
RECIPES FOR BREAKFAST

BREAKFAST TOAST

Preparation time 25 minutes

Servings 1

INGREDIENTS

- ❖ 1 slice / n toast
- ❖ 20 g remoulade
- ❖ 3 g Chives, fresh
- ❖ 20 g zucchini
- ❖ 10 g Soft tomato (s), dried
- ❖ 1 Egg (s), hard-boiled

PREPARATION

1. Toast the slice of bread in the toaster.
2. Pour the tartar sauce into a bowl. Add the chopped chives. Cut the zucchini into slices, then dice and add. Finely dice the tomatoes, place in the bowl and mix everything well.
3. Spread this spread evenly on the toast. Cut the egg into slices using an egg cutter. Drape these on top of the spread so that they overlap and season with salt and pepper.
4. Arrange the breakfast toast on a plate, garnish and serve.

BREAKFAST BURGER

Preparation time 5 minutes

Cooking / Baking time 5 minutes

Servings 1

INGREDIENTS

- ❖ 1 Bread roll (wheat toastie)
- ❖ 1 slice / n Bacon
- ❖ 1 slice / n processed cheese
- ❖ 1 Egg (s)

PREPARATION

1. Cut and bake the toastie. In the meantime, fry 1 egg in the frying ring, fry the bacon in the pan (the egg becomes thicker and round like the toastie in the frying ring). Pour the processed cheese over the egg so that it melts.
2. Pour the slice of fried bacon over it and serve everything together in the toastie.

BAKED TOASTED MUFFINS WITH EGG AND BACON

Preparation time 10 minutes

Cooking / Baking time 30 minutes

Servings 4

INGREDIENTS

- ❖ 3 tsp Thyme, leaves, or 3 sprigs of thyme
- ❖ 4 tbsp olive oil
- ❖ 4 slice / n toast
- ❖ 2 tbsp Mustard medium hot
- ❖ 4 slice / n Breakfast bacon, or bacon
- ❖ 4 m.-large Egg (s)

PREPARATION

1. Preheat the oven to 160 ° C top and bottom heat. If you use thyme sprigs, wash them, shake them dry and pluck the leaves off.
2. Brush four hollows of a muffin tin with the oil. Roll out slices of toast with a rolling pin. Carefully press each slice into the hollows, brush with a little mustard, line with a slice of bacon and sprinkle with thyme. Beat an egg in each toast muffin. Bake the muffins in the oven for 25-30 minutes, until the egg has set.
3. Carefully lift the muffins out of the hollow and serve.

CAPRESE AVOCADO BREAKFAST TOAST

Preparation time 30 minutes

Rest time 25 minutes

Cooking / Baking time 2 minutes

Servings 4

INGREDIENTS

- ❖ 150 g Cherry tomato (s), halved
- ❖ 150 g Mini mozzarella, halved
- ❖ 10 g Basil, fresh, chopped
- ❖ 1 tbsp Olive oil plus 2 teaspoons for marinating or serving
- ❖ 1 Avocado (s), pitted, pulp mashed
- ❖ 4 slice / n loaf
- ❖ 4th Egg (s)
- ❖ salt and pepper

PREPARATION

1. Mix the tomatoes, mozzarella balls, basil and 1 teaspoon olive oil in a bowl. Season with salt and pepper. Cover and let stand for 25 minutes at room temperature.
2. Heat 1 tbsp olive oil in a pan. Fry the eggs in it until the egg white has hardened, 1 - 2 minutes on each side.
3. Toast bread as you like.
4. Spread some avocado on bread, place a fried egg and ¼ of the caprese mixture on top. Do this until you have finished all 4 toasts. Drizzle with a little salt, pepper and olive oil. Serve immediately.

TOAST WITH SMOKED SALMON AND SCRAMBLED EGGS

Preparation time 5 minutes

Servings 2

INGREDIENTS

- ❖ 4 slice / n Toast, white
- ❖ 4 slice / n Salmon, smoked
- ❖ 3 tbsp butter
- ❖ ½ Onion (s), cut into thin rings
- ❖ 3 Egg (s)
- ❖ Something dill
- ❖ Salt and pepper, freshly ground

PREPARATION

1. Toast the bread slices until crispy, spread thinly with butter and top with the smoked salmon.
2. Whisk the eggs with salt and dill and let them set in heated butter while stirring constantly, but do not let them become too firm.
3. Spread the scrambled eggs on the toast, cover each with a couple of onion rings, grind with pepper and serve immediately.

THE BEST BREAKFAST SANDWICH
(HALF ROAST WITH AVOCADO, HALF MONTE CRISTO)

Preparation time 5 minutes

Cooking / Baking time 5 minutes

Servings 2

INGREDIENTS

- ❖ 4 slices of bread with a firm texture
- ❖ 4-6 slices of back bacon
- ❖ 2 eggs
- ❖ 2 slices of Swiss cheese
- ❖ 1 avocado, thinly sliced
- ❖ 2 tbsp. tablespoons mayonnaise
- ❖ Sriracha, to taste
- ❖ Salt pepper
- ❖ 2 tbsp. tablespoons butter divided

PREPARATION

1. In a skillet, heat 1 tbsp. butter over medium high heat. Add the back bacon slices and brown them for 2-3 minutes, then turn them over and continue cooking for 2 minutes. Turn off the heat and set aside.
2. Meanwhile, heat 1 tbsp. of butter over medium heat in another pan. Crack the eggs in, once the pan is hot, taking care to keep some space between them. Leave the eggs to fry without moving them for about 4-5 minutes, until the white is cooked but the yolk is still runny. Turn off the heat and set aside.
3. Toast the bread.
4. Mix the mayonnaise with a little Sriracha sauce to taste, then spread two of the slices of bread.
5. Assemble the sandwiches with the bacon back slices, cheese, egg and avocado. Season with salt and pepper then place the other slice of bread on top.

BREAKFAST SANDWICH WITH EGG,
BLUE CHEESE AND HOLLANDAISE SAUCE

Preparation time 2 minutes

Cooking / Baking time 5 minutes

Servings 4

INGREDIENTS

- ❖ Hollandaise sauce
- ❖ 1/2 cup buttermilk
- ❖ 1 C. tablespoon flour
- ❖ 2 egg yolks
- ❖ 1/2 tsp. Tea finely grated lemon zest
- ❖ 2 tbsp. tablespoon of butter at room temperature
- ❖ Salt to taste
- ❖ Sandwiches
- ❖ eggs (one for each serving)
- ❖ Vinegar
- ❖ Grilled English Muffins
- ❖ Crumbled blue cheese
- ❖ Leftover steak cut into strips
- ❖ Green onion or chopped chives

PREPARATION

1. For the Hollandaise Sauce
2. Whisk buttermilk with flour in a heatproof bowl until smooth.
3. Add the egg yolks and lemon zest.
4. Place the bowl on a pot of simmering water and cook, whisking regularly, until the mixture is heated through and thickened.
5. Add the butter to the mixture and mix well.
6. For the sandwiches
7. Toast the English muffins, add a little cheese, steak and a poached egg. Garnish with sauce and green onions or chives.

QUICK PAPRIKA SCRAMBLED EGG SANDWICH

Preparation time 15 minutes

Cooking / Baking time 10 minutes

Servings 2

INGREDIENTS

- ❖ 1 red pepper
- ❖ 1 Shallot
- ❖ 4th Eggs
- ❖ 50 ml milk
- ❖ 1 tbsp oil
- ❖ 1 teaspoon dried thyme
- ❖ salt
- ❖ pepper
- ❖ 6 slices Whole wheat toast
- ❖ 40 g butter
- ❖ 3 slices middle ages Gouda
- ❖ 1 tbsp Frozen chives rolls

PREPARATION

1. Halve the peppers, clean, wash and cut into bite-sized pieces. Peel and finely dice shallot. Beat the eggs and stir gently with the milk.
2. Heat the oil in a pan. Fry the bell pepper pieces with the shallots and the thyme in them over medium heat for approx. 5 minutes, stirring occasionally. Add the egg and let it set on the bottom of the pan. After 1-2 minutes, occasionally push aside with the spatula until the egg is almost completely set. Season with salt and pepper.
3. Toast the bread and brush with butter, cover 3 slices with the cheese. Spread the scrambled eggs on these slices and sprinkle with the chives. Then open the other slices, cut the bread in half diagonally and serve.

BREAKFAST EMPANADAS

Preparation time 25 minutes

Cooking / Baking time 15 minutes

Servings 6

INGREDIENTS

- ❖ 1/2 recipe of homemade or store-bought pie dough *
- ❖ 5 eggs
- ❖ 2 green onions, thinly sliced
- ❖ 1 cup of chorizo, already cooked, diced or thinly sliced
- ❖ 1/2 cup grated Jalapeño Monterey Jack cheese
- ❖ 2 tbsp. tablespoon of butter
- ❖ 1 egg (for gilding; optional)
- ❖ 1 C. tablespoon milk (for gilding; optional)

PREPARATION

1. Preheat the oven to 425 F.
2. Prepare a baking sheet lined with parchment paper.
3. Break the 5 eggs into a bowl and add salt and pepper. Beat them lightly with a fork.
4. Heat a large skillet over medium high heat, then melt the butter in it.
5. Pour the beaten eggs into the pan, then let them set for about 30 seconds. With a wooden spoon, then start to gently scramble them, until the whites are set. Eggs should not be overcooked, as they will continue to cook in the oven.
6. Turn off the heat and add the green onion. Reserve.
7. On a large floured surface, roll out pie dough to about 1/4 inch (0.6 cm) thickness, also lightly flouring dough and rolling pin.
8. With the rim of a bowl (the one used for the photo was 6 1/2 inches in diameter, or 17 cm), mark circles of dough, then cut the dough, if necessary, using a knife. Remove excess dough so that only the circles remain on the work surface. The excess dough can then be gathered into a ball and then rolled out again.

9. Top each round of dough in the middle with the equivalent of 1/4 cup of eggs, 6 pieces or small slices of chorizo and 1 Tbsp. grated cheese. Be careful to leave the rim of the dough circle empty.

10. Holding the filling with one hand so it does not spill out, close each circle of dough with the other hand to form a half moon.

11. Line up the edges, then press all the way around the half-moon with a fork, to better seal the empanadas. Place the empanadas on the baking sheet.

12. In a small bowl, break another egg and add the milk. Beat lightly with a fork.

13. Brush each empanada with the gilding.

14. Bake until the empanadas are golden brown, about 12 to 15 minutes.

15. Serve hot with salsa, sour cream or guacamole .

SCRAMBLED EGG AND MUSHROOM BURRITO

Preparation time 5 minutes

Cooking / Baking time 10 minutes

Servings 4

INGREDIENTS

- ❖ 2 original POM
- ❖ 3 eggs
- ❖ 1/4 tsp. tsp (1 mL) salt and pepper 2 tbsp. (30 mL) olive oil
- ❖ 1 cup (250 mL) chopped brown mushrooms
- ❖ 4 tbsp. tsp (20 mL) chives, finely chopped
- ❖ 1/4 cup (60 mL) crumbled goat cheese

PREPARATION

1. Whisk the eggs, salt and pepper; Reserve. Heat half the oil in an 8-inch (20 cm) non-stick frying pan over medium heat; cook mushrooms 4 to 6 minutes or until softened.
2. Add the rest of the oil to the pan and heat through; pour in the egg mixture. Cook 3 to 4 minutes or until egg mixture sets and begins to scramble; stir in the chives.
3. Place tortillas on a clean surface; top evenly with scrambled egg and goat cheese mixture. Fold the bottom of the tortillas over the filling, then fold down the sides and roll up tight.

PANCAKES RECIPES
FOR BREAKFAST

JULIA ROSS

THIN PANCAKES FOR BREAKFAST

Preparation time 10 minutes

Cooking / Baking time 25 minutes

Servings 14

INGREDIENTS

- ❖ 150 g (1 cup) unbleached all-purpose flour
- ❖ 30 ml (2 tbsp.) Sugar
- ❖ 1 pinch of salt
- ❖ 2 eggs
- ❖ 375 ml (1 ½ cup) milk
- ❖ 1/2 teaspoon (2.5 ml) vanilla extract
- ❖ 15 ml (1 tbsp.) Unsalted butter, melted
- ❖ Softened butter, for cooking

PREPARATION

1. In a bowl, combine the flour, sugar and salt. Add the eggs, 125 ml (½ cup) of the milk and the vanilla then mix well with the whisk until the dough is smooth and homogeneous. Gradually add the remaining milk while stirring. Incorporate the melted butter.
2. Heat a non - stick pan about 23 cm (9 inches) in diameter over medium heat. When the pan is hot, brush with butter with a brush .
3. For each pancake, pour about 45 ml (3 tbsp.) Of batter in the center of the pan. As you rotate the pan, try to spread the dough evenly to cover the entire bottom. When the rim peels off easily and begins to brown, it's time to flip the pancake with a spatula . Continue cooking for 10 seconds then remove from the pan.
4. Place the cooked pancakes on a plate as you go. Cover with foil to prevent them from drying out. Keep warm. Delicious with maple syrup or blueberry sauce.

94

BREAKFAST PANCAKES

Preparation time 10 minutes

Cooking / Baking time 5 minutes

Servings 4

PREPARATION

- ❖ 250 g Flour
- ❖ 3Eggs
- ❖ 60 g Sugar
- ❖ 25 cl Milk
- ❖ 1 sachet Baking powder

PREPARATION

1. In a bowl, mix the milk with the eggs then add a pinch of salt and sugar.
2. Add the flour and the sifted yeast, then mix with a whisk until a soft dough is obtained.
3. Place a ladle in a hot pan with a knob of butter and cook for 2 minutes per side then repeat the operation.

SOFT PANCAKES FOR BREAKFAST

Preparation time 5 minutes

Cooking / Baking time 45 minutes

Servings 6

INGREDIENTS

- ❖ Baking powder
- ❖ 2 sachets of baking powder
- ❖ Butter
- ❖ 100 g of melted butter
- ❖ Milk
- ❖ 60 cl of milk
- ❖ Salt or fine salt
- ❖ 0.5 tsp. to c. salt or fine salt
- ❖ Egg
- ❖ 2 eggs
- ❖ Sugar
- ❖ 40g sugar
- ❖ Flour
- ❖ 400 g flour

PREPARATION

1. In a container, put the flour, sugar, salt, baking powder, lightly beaten eggs. Add the milk and then the melted butter. Mix everything well with a whisk.
2. Heat a buttered pan. Place a tablespoon of your dough on the pan (and so on), and cook on both sides.
3. Pancakes are eaten with maple syrup, but you can also eat them with jam, honey or even spread.

COCONUT FLOUR PANCAKE

Preparation time 10 minutes

Cooking / Baking time 20 minutes

Servings 12

INGREDIENTS

- ❖ 50 g coconut flour
- ❖ 100 g small spelled flour
- ❖ 2 eggs
- ❖ 350 g 9.5% coconut milk

PREPARATION

1. Mix the eggs and flour
2. Mix with coconut milk
3. Cook in a pancake pan. It is possible to cook them 3 by 3.

BLUEBERRY BREAKFAST PANCAKES

Preparation time 25 minutes

Cooking / Baking time 15 minutes

Servings 10

Ingredients

- ❖ Blueberries 125 g
- ❖ heavy cream 125 g
- ❖ eggs 2
- ❖ Butter 5 c. coffee
- ❖ Milk 2 tbsp. soup
- ❖ Maple syrup
- ❖ 4 tbsp. soup
- ❖ flour for pastry 125 g
- ❖ brown sugar
- ❖ 2 tbsp. soup
- ❖ baking powder 1 sachets
- ❖ vanilla flavor 0.5 tubes
- ❖ salt
- ❖ 1 pinch

PREPARATION

1. Place the egg yolks, heavy cream, milk, brown sugar, vanilla flavoring, baking powder and salt in a large bowl. Beat with an electric mixer.
2. Gently mix the flour and half of the blueberries with your hands in another bowl. Incorporate this mixture into the egg mixture without damaging the blueberries, which must remain whole.
3. Whip the egg whites until stiff. Gently fold them into the blueberry paste with a spatula. Cover with a damp kitchen towel and let stand for 15 minutes at room temperature.
4. Melt 1 tbsp. of butter in a pan and cook 2 small pancakes (pour 2 tablespoons of batter per pancake). Allow 1 to 2 minutes of cooking on each side to obtain golden pancakes. Make 10 pancakes in total.

WAFFLE RECIPES
FOR BREAKFAST

BREAKFAST WAFFLE WITH FRIED EGG, RAW HAM AND GOAT CHEESE

Preparation time 30 minutes

Cooking / Baking time 15 minutes

Servings 4

INGREDIENTS

- ❖ 4 eggs
- ❖ 4 slices of raw ham
- ❖ 1 small ball of mild goat cheese
- ❖ a handful of watercress , passed under water
- ❖ salt and pepper
- ❖ For the waffles
- ❖ g fresh yeast
- ❖ 2 dl lukewarm water
- ❖ 3 eggs
- ❖ 1 sachet of vanilla sugar
- ❖ 250g of flour
- ❖ 2 dl lukewarm milk
- ❖ 100 g of melted butter

PREPARATION

1. Dilute the yeast in lukewarm water.
2. Separate the egg whites from the yolks.
3. Beat the eggs with the vanilla sugar.
4. Mix the flour with the lukewarm milk, mix in the melted butter and then the egg yolks. Stir until you get a smooth mixture and add the yeast mixture to it.
5. Stir again until you obtain a smooth mixture and incorporate the egg whites.
6. Let the dough rise, covered, for 20 minutes in a warm place.
7. Bake the waffles in a large grid waffle iron until they are a nice brown color.
8. Fry 4 eggs, salt and pepper. Crumble the goat cheese.

9. Place a fried egg on a waffle, cover with a slice of ham and a little goat cheese, garnish with a little watercress.

OATMEAL BUTTERMILK WAFFLES

Preparation time 10 minutes

Cooking / Baking time 50 minutes

Servings 6

INGREDIENTS

- ❖ 1 cup of flour (250 ml)
- ❖ 1 1/2 cups quick oats (375 mL)
- ❖ 3 tbsp. to s. sugar (30 mL)
- ❖ 2 tbsp. to c. baking powder (10 ml)
- ❖ 1 tbsp. to c. baking soda (5 mL)
- ❖ 1/2 tsp. to c. salt (2.5 mL)
- ❖ 2 cups of buttermilk (500 ml)
- ❖ 4 large eggs
- ❖ 1 stick of unsalted butter , melted and cooled (125 mL)
- ❖ 1 tbsp. to c. pure vanilla extract (5 ml)

PREPARATION

1. In a large bowl, whisk together the flour, oats, sugar, baking powder, baking soda and salt.
2. In a small bowl, whisk together buttermilk, eggs, butter and vanilla.
3. Add the buttermilk mixture to the dry ingredients, stirring until well combined. Let the dough rest while the waffle iron heats up.
4. Spray the waffle iron with cooking spray.
5. Pour the batter * into the waffle iron, close the lid and bake until the waffle is golden brown and easily peels off the waffle iron. Repeat with the rest of the dough.
6. Waffles should be served immediately or can be kept warm in a low heat oven (200 ° F) until they are all done.
7. Serve with butter and maple syrup or yogurt and fresh fruit.

BASIC WAFFLE BATTER RECIPE

Preparation time 30 minutes

Cooking / Baking time 10 minutes

Servings 5

INGREDIENTS

- ❖ 125 G Butter (soft)
- ❖ 75 G Granulated sugar
- ❖ 3 Pc Eggs
- ❖ 250 G Flour
- ❖ 2 TL Baking powder (coated)
- ❖ 1 Pk vanilla sugar
- ❖ 200 mlb milk

PREPARATION

1. For the basic waffle batter recipe, first put the softened butter in a bowl. Add the granulated sugar and stir well with a whisk. Add the eggs, mix everything well again.
2. Then stir in the flour, baking powder, vanilla sugar and milk until a creamy, smooth dough is formed.
3. Preheat the waffle iron and brush well with butter. Then use a scoop to pour the batter into the waffle iron in portions. Close the waffle iron and fry golden yellow waffles.

BANANA WAFFLES

Preparation time 20 minutes

Cooking / Baking time 10 minutes

Servings 4

INGREDIENTS

- ❖ 1 Pc banana
- ❖ 200 G Flour
- ❖ 1 Pk baking powder
- ❖ 1 Pk vanilla sugar
- ❖ 3 Pc Eggs
- ❖ 1 shot Mineral water
- ❖ 125 G Butter (soft)
- ❖ 50 G Icing sugar

PREPARATION

1. For the banana waffles, first peel the banana, cut into pieces and puree with the hand blender.
2. For the dough, put the flour, baking powder, sugar, eggs, water and butter in a bowl and knead the dough with a mixer, add the banana mixture and stir vigorously again.
3. Pour the batter into the hot waffle iron in portions and bake golden brown waffles.

WHOLEGRAIN WAFFLES

Preparation time 20 minutes

Cooking / Baking time 60 minutes

Servings 4

INGREDIENTS

- ❖ 2 Tbsp Maple, agave or fruit syrup
- ❖ 50 G Margarine, dairy-free
- ❖ 1 prize salt
- ❖ 250 ml water
- ❖ 200 G Wheat, spelled, buckwheat or corn
- ❖ 1 TL cinnamon

PREPARATION

1. Finely grind the grain and mix with the salt and cinnamon.
2. Mix the margarine with the maple, agave or fruit syrup, the wholemeal flour and the water to form a thick dough and cover it and let it soak for about 30-60 minutes.
3. Then stir well again, preheat the waffle iron and bake four waffles one after the other.

YOGURT VANILLA WAFFLES

Preparation time 5 minutes

Cooking / Baking time 15 minutes

Servings 8

INGREDIENTS

- ❖ 350 G Natural yoghurt
- ❖ 6th Pc Eggs
- ❖ 350 G Flour
- ❖ 1 Pk baking powder
- ❖ 1 Pk Vanilla pudding powder
- ❖ 125 ml Vegetable oil
- ❖ 3 Tbsp sugar
- ❖ 3 Tbsp Icing sugar (for sprinkling)

PREPARATION

1. Mix the flour with the baking powder and the vanilla pudding powder.
2. Mix the eggs with the oil and yoghurt and stir in the flour mixture.
3. Bake golden yellow waffles from the batter in the waffle iron in portions, dust with icing sugar after baking.

FRENCH TOAST MUFFINS
RECIPES FOR BREAKFAST

EGG BENEDICT MUFFINS

Preparation time 10 minutes

Cooking / Baking time 15 minutes

Servings 4

INGREDIENTS

Hollandaise sauce

- ❖ 1 egg
- ❖ 100 g Butter
- ❖ Fine salt
- ❖ Lemon

Garnish ingredients

- ❖ 2 eggs
- ❖ 1/2 tsp. vinegar
- ❖ 2 English muffins, cut in half
- ❖ 2 slices of ham
- ❖ 1/2 tomato
- ❖ 2 sprigs of chives

PREPARATION

1. Heat a double boiler for the hollandaise sauce.
2. Poach the 2 eggs in simmering water with the vinegar, to facilitate coagulation.
3. Cut the muffins in half and toast them.
4. Put the egg yolk in a saucepan. Dissolve with a tablespoon of cold water.
5. Add the butter while whisking.
6. Place in the hot bain-marie and whisk until you obtain a frothy and light cream.
7. When the poached eggs are cooked, place them on a paper towel to soak up the excess water.
8. Slice the tomatoes.

9. To assemble: place the tomato on one side of a muffin, the poached egg, the ham, the Hollandaise sauce and cut the chives on top with scissors. Cover the other side of the muffin and serve immediately.

ENGLISH MUFFINS

Preparation time 15 minutes

Rest time 2hours

Cooking / Baking time 10 minutes

Servings 11

INGREDIENTS

- ❖ 250 grams of flour (a little more during kneading)
- ❖ 1 teaspoon of sugar
- ❖ 1/2 teaspoon of salt
- ❖ 1 sachet of dehydrated baker's yeast
- ❖ 40 grams of butter
- ❖ 160 ml milk
- ❖ Wheat semolina

PREPARATION

1. In a bowl or a glass put the yeast, sugar and lukewarm milk. Mix then let the yeast rehydrate for 10 minutes.
2. In a bowl, combine the flour, salt and butter.
3. Add the yeast-milk mixture.
4. Knead for 5 minutes, add flour if necessary, so that it comes off the hand.
5. Stop after obtaining a smooth paste.
6. Cover the bowl with a tea towel for 1 hour. The dough must double in volume.
7. Flour the work surface and spread to a thickness of about 1 cm.
8. Then cut circles with a cookie cutter or a glass, about 7 to 10 cm in diameter. Especially do not turn, just push in and release.
9. Place the circles on baking paper and sprinkle each side with wheat semolina.
10. Cover with a tea towel and let stand another 1 hour, to double in size.
11. Heat a frying pan over low heat without fat.
12. Place the muffins and cook for 5 minutes on each side, to obtain a nice golden color.

FRENCH TOAST

Preparation time 5 minutes

Cooking / Baking time 5 minutes

Servings 2

INGREDIENTS

- ❖ 2 slices of bread
- ❖ 3 eggs
- ❖ Granulated sugar

PREPARATION

1. Break the eggs into the bowl and beat them. Add a little sugar and milk.
2. Pour the mixture into the deep plate and place the slice of bread on it.
3. Press the slice of bread for a few seconds.
4. Turn the slice over and start the operation again.
5. Put a piece of butter in the hot pan.
6. Once the butter has melted, place the slice of bread using the spatula and leave to brown for a few minutes.
7. Turn the slice of bread over and repeat the operation.

TRIO OF MINI FRENCH BREADS IN THE OVEN

Preparation time 10 minutes

Cooking / Baking time 15 minutes

Servings 12

INGREDIENTS

- ❖ Sugar
- ❖ 50 g sugar
- ❖ Dark chocolate
- ❖ 35 g of crushed dark chocolate
- ❖ Milk
- ❖ 25 cl of milk
- ❖ Raspberry
- ❖ 15 raspberries
- ❖ Bread
- ❖ 7 slices of bread or 200g of bread
- ❖ Egg
- ❖ 3 eggs
- ❖ Red fruit
- ❖ 1 large handful of red fruits
- ❖ Vanilla extract or liquid vanilla
- ❖ 0.5 tsp. to c. vanilla extract or liquid vanilla
- ❖ Brown cane sugar or brown sugar
- ❖ Brown cane sugar or brown sugar for the finish
- ❖ Oil
- ❖ Oil for the mold

PREPARATION

1. In a bowl, beat the eggs with the sugar.
2. Add the milk and vanilla and whisk.
3. Cut the bread into cubes, without removing the crust.

4. Soak the bread in the milk mixture and let stand for 10 minutes. Oil a muffin pan.

5. Half-fill the muffin pan with the soaked bread, taking in liquid each time.

6. Add 3 raspberries in 5 indentations.

7. Add 2 teaspoons of red berries in 4 imprints.

8. Add 3-4 pieces of chocolate in 3 imprints.

9. Cover the filling with the rest of the preparation.

10. Sprinkle with brown sugar.

11. Tamp each French toast with the back of a large spoon.

12. Bake for about twenty minutes in a preheated 170 ° C oven. The top should be golden brown. Wait 5 minutes then unmold using a large spoon. These mini French toast are served warm, at room temperature or cold.

FRENCH TOAST FOR A FULL BREAKFAST

Preparation time 5 minutes

Cooking / Baking time 5 minutes

Servings 6

INGREDIENTS

- ❖ Milk
- ❖ 30 cl of milk
- ❖ Egg
- ❖ 2 eggs
- ❖ Sugar
- ❖ 1 tablespoon of sugar (or brown sugar)
- ❖ Vanilla sugar
- ❖ 2 sachets of vanilla sugar
- ❖ 6 slices of slightly stale country bread (or brioche)

PREPARATION

1. Pour the milk into a deep plate. Add the vanilla sugar and powdered sugar. Stir to dissolve the sugar.
2. Beat the eggs and put them in another deep plate.
3. Dip the slices of bread in the milk to soak them lightly then in the beaten egg.
4. Cook the French toast in a pan with a little butter
5. Return after a few minutes. The French toast is ready when both sides are golden.
6. Serve hot and sprinkled with icing sugar.

BREAD RECIPES
FOR BREAKFAST

PEASANT BREAD

Preparation time 15 minutes

Rest time 1hour

Cooking / Baking time 40 minutes

Servings 4

INGREDIENTS

- ❖ flour for white bread250 g
- ❖ flour (for gray bread)300 g
- ❖ Brown sugar1 tbsp
- ❖ salt½ tsp
- ❖ baker's yeast (dehydrated)1.5 tsp
- ❖ water (spring, lukewarm)30 cl
- ❖ soft butter25 g

PREPARATION

1. Pour the two flours with the yeast, sugar and salt in a bowl. Mix. Dig a well in the center and pour in the water and then the butter in pieces.
2. Mix by gradually incorporating the flour then knead the dough, 10 minutes, until it is elastic. Add more flour if it is too sticky.
3. Cover with a damp towel and let rise, 45 minutes to 1 hour, warm: the dough should have doubled in volume.
4. Preheat the oven to 200 ° C. Brown the bread for 40 minutes in a hot oven.
5. Reserve it on a rack. Let it cool completely before cutting it.

BANANA BREAD

Preparation time 30 minutes

Cooking / Baking time 45 minutes

Servings 4

INGREDIENTS

- ❖ bananas (small)3
- ❖ ground hazelnuts (or almond powder)50 g
- ❖ butter (+ extra)124 g
- ❖ eggs3
- ❖ sugar125 g
- ❖ flour200 g
- ❖ baking powder½ bag
- ❖ lemon juice2 tbsp
- ❖ salt1 pinch

PREPARATION

1. Butter a cake tin, then sprinkle it with hazelnut (or almond) powder. Book. Preheat the oven to 180 ° C.
2. Whisk together the butter and sugar until you obtain a frothy mixture.
3. Put a pinch of salt in the egg whites and beat them until stiff. Incorporate the yolks one by one into the butter / sugar mixture. Whisk until you obtain a frothy mass.
4. Mix the flour, baking powder and hazelnut (or almond) powder. Sift everything over the butter / sugar mixture. Mix to obtain a very smooth paste.
5. Crush the flesh of the bananas. Add the lemon juice. Incorporate everything into the dough.
6. Carefully incorporate the snow whites into the preparation.
7. Pour the batter into the mold. Smooth on the surface. Cook for 45 minutes. Unmold and let cool on a rack.

NUT BREAD

Preparation time 25 minutes

Rest time 45 minutes

Cooking / Baking time 35 minutes

Servings 4

INGREDIENTS

- ❖ flour for white bread450 g
- ❖ warm milk)25 cl
- ❖ baker's yeast (dehydrated)1 tsp
- ❖ liquid honey2 tbsp
- ❖ egg1
- ❖ soft butter1 tbsp
- ❖ salt½ tsp
- ❖ chopped nuts100 g

PREPARATION

1. Sift the flour over a large bowl; dig a well in the center. Mix the milk with the yeast and honey in a bowl and pour into the well.
2. Add the beaten egg and the butter, mix then add the salt and knead, 15 minutes, into a soft dough. Cover and let rise, 45 minutes, warm.
3. Knead again, incorporating the chopped nuts.
4. Bring back into a ball, cover again and let rise, 30 minutes, warm.
5. Preheat the oven to 200 ° C. Place the dough on a baking sheet lined with baking paper or in a buttered loaf pan. Bake for 35 minutes in a hot oven.

RAISIN BREAD

Preparation time 25 minutes

Rest time 45minutes

Cooking / Baking time 35 minutes

Servings 4

INGREDIENTS

- ❖ flour for white bread450 g
- ❖ warm milk)25 cl
- ❖ liquid honey2 tbsp
- ❖ baker's yeast (dehydrated)1 tsp
- ❖ egg1
- ❖ Butter1 tbsp
- ❖ salt½ tsp
- ❖ raisins100 g

PREPARATION

1. Sift the flour over a large bowl, dig a well in the center. Mix the milk with the yeast and honey in a bowl and pour into the well.
2. Add the beaten egg and the butter, mix then add the salt and knead, 15 minutes, into a soft dough. Cover and let rise, 45 minutes, warm.
3. Knead again, incorporating the raisins.
4. Bring back into a ball, cover again and let rise, 30 minutes, warm.
5. Preheat the oven to 200 ° C. Place the dough on a baking sheet lined with baking paper or in a buttered loaf pan. Bake for 35 minutes in a hot oven.

CHOCOLATE BREAD

Preparation time 30 minutes

Rest time 30

Cooking / Baking time 35 minutes

Servings 4

INGREDIENTS

- ❖ flour for white bread450 g
- ❖ warm milk)25 cl
- ❖ baker's yeast (dehydrated)1 tsp
- ❖ liquid honey2 tbsp
- ❖ egg1
- ❖ soft butter (+ extra for the mold)1 tbsp
- ❖ salt½ tsp
- ❖ dark chocolate chips100 g

PREPARATION

1. Sift the flour over a large bowl and dig a well in the center. Mix the milk with the yeast and the honey then pour everything into the well.
2. Add the beaten egg and the butter, mix then add the salt and knead, 15 minutes, into soft dough.
3. Bring it back into a ball, cover and let rise, 45 minutes, warm.
4. Knead again for a few minutes then incorporate the chocolate chips. Cover and let rise again, 30 minutes, warm.
5. Preheat the oven to 200 ° C. Place the dough on a baking sheet lined with baking paper or in a buttered loaf pan. Bake for 35 minutes in a hot oven.

PASTRIES RECIPES
FOR BREAKFAST

PIZZA BUN

Preparation time 40 minutes

Rest time 30

Cooking / Baking time 20 minutes

Servings 4

INGREDIENTS

- ❖ 300 g wheat flour
- ❖ 1 pck. Dry yeast
- ❖ 1 level tsp sugar
- ❖ 1 level tsp salt
- ❖ 2 tbsp olive oil
- ❖ 200 ml water
- ❖ 140 g Canned corn
- ❖ 125 g Cheese (whole)
- ❖ 200 g Red pesto

PREPARATION

1. In a mixing bowl, mix 300 g wheat flour with 1 packet of dry yeast .
2. Add 1 level teaspoon sugar , 1 level teaspoon salt , 1 tablespoon olive oil and 200 ml water (lukewarm) .
3. With the dough hook mixer you knead all the ingredients then 5 min. Long to a smooth
4. Cover the mixing bowl with a tea towel and place the batter in a warm place . Let it go there for about 30 minutes until it has doubled in size.
5. Cover a baking sheet with a sheet of parchment paper .
6. Now you can preheat the oven to 200 ° C top and bottom heat (180 ° C convection) . So it has the right temperature when you put the pizza rolls in the oven.
7. Drain 140g of corn in a colander .
8. Now cut 125 g cheese (in one piece) on a board with a small, sharp knife into 16 cubes .
9. When your dough is done, shape it into a roll and cut 16 pieces .
10. Now shape all the pieces of dough into balls .

11. Use a rolling pin to roll your balls into small, round cakes.

12. Now it's time to fill. Grab 200 g of pesto and coat your flatbreads well with it. It's best to leave some space to the edge.

13. Now put a cheese cube on each flat cake and then sprinkle something on everythingCorn .

14. Next, you close the pizza rolls by lifting the edges and pressing them together well at the top.

15. Place your buns, pressed side down, on your prepared baking sheet. If all of the rolls don't fit on the tray, bake one half first and then the other half.

16. Now mix 1 tablespoon of olive oil with 1 level teaspoon of pizza spice in a small bowl.

17. Brush your pizza rolls with the olive oil mixture. This works particularly well with a pastry brush.

18. Off to the oven with the pizza rolls. You now have to bake for 20 minutes in the middle of the oven.

19. When your rolls are done baked, take them out of the oven.

20. Your pizza rolls are ready to be eaten. They taste best when they are still warm - bon appetite!

SAVORY YEAST SUN

Preparation time 55 minutes

Rest time 1hour 10 minutes

Cooking / Baking time 20 minutes

Servings 4

INGREDIENTS

- ❖ 515 g wheat flour
- ❖ 1 pck. Dry yeast
- ❖ 7 g salt
- ❖ 1 level tsp sugar
- ❖ 80 g butter
- ❖ 100 g Quark
- ❖ 215 ml milk
- ❖ 2 Eggs (size M)
- ❖ 125 g Crème fraîche with fresh herbs
- ❖ 200 g grated cheese
- ❖ 50 g salami
- ❖ 50 g Cooked ham (sliced)
- ❖ Something ground pepper
- ❖ 2 tbsp Sunflower seeds
- ❖ 1 level tsp Pizza seasoning

PREPARATION

1. Let's start preparing the dough for the Yeast Sun: mix 500 g wheat flour and 1 packet of dry yeast in a mixing bowl.
2. Add 1 level teaspoon salt, 1 level teaspoon sugar and 80 g butter.
3. Add 100 g quark and 200 ml milk to the mixing bowl.
4. Separate 1 egg (size M) and add the egg white to the mixing bowl. The egg yolk you give in a small bowl.

5. Now add 1 tablespoon of milk to the egg yolk and stir everything into a uniform mass. Put the egg yolk and milk mixture aside for now.

6. Then knead the ingredients in the mixing bowl with the dough hook of the mixer for about 5 minutes to form a smooth dough.

7. Cover the dough with a tea towel and let the dough rise for about 30 minutes in a warm place.

8. You can prepare the filling while the dough is rising. Put 125 g of crème fraîche with fresh herbs, 1 egg (size M) and 150 g of grated cheese in a mixing bowl .

9. Wash 1 bell pepper and use a small, sharp knife to remove the stalk and seeds on a board

10. Then cut the peppers into small cubes.

11. Take 50 g salami and 50 g cooked ham and cut these ingredients into small pieces.

12. Put everything in the mixing bowl and season it with some ground pepper and a pinch of salt. Then mix everything once with a tablespoon.

13. Prepare a baking sheet and 2 sheets of baking paper so that your yeast sun can be removed more easily from the baking sheet later.

14. Once the dough has risen, dust some wheat flour into the bowl, then place the dough on the work surface. The flour will keep your dough from sticking to your work surface.

15. Knead the dough briefly with your hands again and then shape it into a roll.

16. Now use a small, sharp knife to divide the roll into 4 equal pieces.

17. Then shape all the pieces of dough into balls.

18. Roll two balls with a rolling pin to about 35 cm round cakes, and put them on the prepared baking sheet with the baking paper.

19. Now it's time to fill. Take the prepared filling and divide half of each between two flat cakes.

20. Spread the filling evenly with the tablespoon. Make sure you leave about 2 cm to the edge.

21. Now use a brush to help and brush the edge of the flatbreads with the egg yolk and milk mixture you set aside. Make sure that you leave a little of the mixture as you will need it again later to coat your dough.

22. Now use the rolling pin to roll out the other two cakes.

23. Now carefully place the two flat cakes on top of the filling.

24. Next, roll the rolling pin carefully from the center outwards towards the edge so that the excess air can escape.

25. Then you press the edge together firmly so that your filling cannot run out later during baking.

26. Place a glass in the center of your yeast dough. Then cut the dough outwards into 12 equal pieces with a pizza roller.

27. Now remove the glass again and carefully twist each piece of dough in itself.

28. Then brush your piquant yeast sun with the remaining egg yolk and milk mixture. The best thing to do is to use a brush again   .

29. Now mix 50 g of grated cheese, 2 tablespoons of sunflower seeds with 1 level teaspoon of pizza seasoning in a small bowl.

30. Then spread the mixture evenly over the two flat cakes.

31. Place your yeast sun in a warm place and let it go again for 30 minutes.

32. So that the oven is hot when your yeast sun is ready to bake, preheat it to 200 ° C top and bottom heat (180 ° C convection).

33. Now the yeast sun has to go for about20 minutes in the oven. It works best if you place it in the middle of your oven.

34. After the baking time, you take your yeast sun out of the oven and let it cool down on a wire rack for about 10 minutes. Then you can also bake your second yeast sun. Enojy your meal!

PARTY BREAD WREATH

Preparation time 50 minutes

Rest time 1 hour 35 minutes

Cooking / Baking time 15 minutes

Servings 4

INGREDIENTS

- ❖ 500 g Spelled flour (type 1050)
- ❖ 1 pck Dry yeast
- ❖ 1 level tsp salt
- ❖ 1 level tsp sugar
- ❖ 80 g butter
- ❖ 100 g Quark
- ❖ 215 ml milk
- ❖ Egg (size M)
- ❖ 100 g roasted peppers skinless (in a glass)
- ❖ 100 g Raw ham (sliced)
- ❖ Something wheat flour
- ❖ 10 g frozen herbs
- ❖ 50 g Creme fraiche Cheese
- ❖ 20 g Poppy
- ❖ 20 g sesame
- ❖ 20 g Sunflower seeds
- ❖ 30 g grated cheese

PREPARATION

1. Mix 500 g spelled flour (type 1050) and 1 packet of dry yeast in a mixing bowl.
2. Add 1 level teaspoon salt, 1 level teaspoon sugar and 80 g butter.
3. Add 100 g of quark and 200 ml of milk.
4. Separate 1 egg (size M) and add the egg white to the mixing bowl. The egg yolk you give in a small bowl.

5. Add 1 tablespoon of milk to the egg yolk, stir everything and set it aside for later.

6. Knead all ingredients in the mixing bowl with the dough hook of the mixer for 5 minutes to form dough.

7. Cover the dough with a tea towel and let it rise for at least 30 minutes.

8. So that the oven is hot when the bread is ready to bake, preheat it to 200 ° C top and bottom heat (180 ° C convection).

9. Now you can also prepare the filling. To do this, drain 100 g of roasted peppers on a sieve.

10. Parts 100 g raw ham with a small sharp knife on a small board into small portions

11. When the roasted bell peppers have drained well, use a small, sharp knife to cut them into small portions.

12. Prepare a baking sheet with a sheet of parchment paper.

13. Once the dough has risen, dust some wheat flour into the bowl, then place the dough on the work surface.

14. Knead the dough again briefly and then shape it into a roll.

15. Divide the roll into 5 equal pieces.

16. Knead a piece of dough with 10 g of frozen herbs.

17. Now shape the dough pieces into a roll and divide them into 4 pieces each.

18. Now shape all the pieces of dough into balls.

19. Use a rolling pin to roll your balls into small, round cakes.

20. Now it's time to fill. Grab 50 g of crème fraîche and add about half a teaspoon to the center of your flat cakes.

21. Now spread the roasted peppers on each flatbread.

22. Now you distribute the prepared raw ham .

23. Next you close the buns by lifting the edges and pressing them together well at the top.

24. Place your buns, pressed side down, in a wreath on the prepared baking sheet.

25. Use a brush to brush the top of the buns with the egg yolk milk you set aside.

26. Sprinkle 4 rolls with 20 g poppy seeds, 20 g sesame seeds, 20 g sunflower seeds and 30 g grated cheese.

27. Let the bread wreath rise for another 30 minutes in a warm place.

28. Now put the rolls in the oven for about 15 minute. They'll work best if you put them in the center of your oven.

29. After baking, let the party bread wreath cool down on a wire rack for another 30 minutes. Then it's ready to eat - bon appetit!

SAVOURY MUFFINS

Preparation time 20 minutes

Rest time 10 minutes

Cooking / Baking time 25 minutes

Servings 6

INGREDIENTS

- ❖ Something butter
- ❖ 265 g wheat flour
- ❖ 100 g Camembert
- ❖ 100 g dried plums
- ❖ 3 level tsp baking powder
- ❖ teaspoon salt
- ❖ 4 tbsp olive oil
- ❖ pinch ground pepper
- ❖ 125 g Crème fraîche with fresh herbs
- ❖ Egg (size M)
- ❖ 100 ml water
- ❖ 50 g Ham cubes

PREPARATION

1. So that your muffins can be easily removed from the mold after baking, you first grease your muffin tin with a little butter . This works best with a pastry brush or some kitchen paper . Now sprinkle some wheat flour into the mold and distribute it by twisting and knocking. You pour the excess flour out of the mold.

2. Preheat your oven to 180 ° C top and bottom heat (160 ° C convection) , then it has the right temperature when the muffins are ready to bake.

3. Now you can continue with the preparations for your dough: cut 100 g camembert and 100 g dried plums into small pieces on a board with a small, sharp knife .

4. Then put 250 g of wheat flour and 3 level teaspoons of baking powder in a mixing bowl . Mix the two briefly with a spoon.

5. Now add 1 teaspoon of salt , 4 tablespoons of olive oil , 1 pinch of ground pepper and 125 g of crème fraîche with fresh herbs to your mixing bowl .

6. Finally, add 1 egg (size M) and 100 ml of water .

7. Then stir everything with the stirrers of the mixer for about 2 minutes to a smooth dough.

8. Now all you have to do is stir in the finely chopped camembert , the dried plums and 50 g diced ham .

9. Then you distribute your dough on the prepared muffin tray . It is best to take two tablespoons and spread the dough into the molds with one spoon from the other.

10. Next, you slide your muffins into your oven. You have to bake for about 25 minutes . They work best if you place the tray in the middle of the oven.

11. After the baking time, take the muffin tin out of the oven. Then carefully remove the muffins from the mold with a simple knife, place them on a wire rack and let them cool for 10 minutes . Then you can eat them already lukewarm - enjoy them!

RAISIN BUTTER MARES

Preparation time 15 minutes

Cooking / Baking time 15 minutes

Servings 10

INGREDIENTS

For the loaf pan (25 x 11 cm):

- ❖ Something fat

Yeast dough:

- ❖ 250 ml milk
- ❖ 50 g butter
- ❖ 500 g Wheat flour type 550 or 405
- ❖ 1 cube fresh yeast
- ❖ 2 Tea spoons sugar
- ❖ ½ tsp salt
- ❖ Egg (size M)
- ❖ 100-200 g Raisins

For painting:

- ❖ Something milk

PREPARATION

1. Warm the milk and melt the butter in it. Put the flour in a mixing bowl. Crumble the yeast on top. Add the rest of the ingredients - except raisins - and process everything with a mixer (dough hook) first on the lowest, then on the highest level in about 5 minutes to a smooth dough. Finally knead in the raisins. Cover and let the dough rise in a warm place until it has visibly enlarged.
2. Grease the loaf pan. Preheat oven.
3. Top / bottom heating around 180 ° C
4. Hot air around 160 ° C

5. Knead the dough well again on a lightly floured work surface and shape into a roll about 25 cm long. Put the dough in the loaf pan and let rise, covered, until it has visibly enlarged. Brush the dough with milk and cut into the length about 1 cm deep. Put the tin on the wire rack in the oven.

6. Let the raisin mares stand on a wire rack for about 10 minutes. Then loosen with a knife, fall out of the mold and let cool.

WHOLE GRAIN CROISSANTS

Preparation time 1hour minutes

Rest 1hour

Cooking / Baking time 15 minutes

Servings 6

INGREDIENTS

For the baking sheet:

- ❖ Baking sheet
- ❖ Parchment paper

Danish pastry for croissants:

- ❖ 300 g cold butter
- ❖ 600 g Whole wheat flour
- ❖ 2 pck. dry yeast
- ❖ 425 ml cold water
- ❖ 25 g soft butter
- ❖ about 1 tsp salt
- ❖ 60 g sugar

For brushing and sprinkling:

- ❖ about 1 Egg (size M)
- ❖ about 50 g Kernels mix, e.g. B. flax seeds, sunflower seeds, pumpkin seeds, sesame seeds

PREPARATION

1. Press cold butter between foil or a cut freezer bag to a square (approx. 25 x 25 cm) and let it solidify again in the refrigerator.
2. Put whole wheat flour in a mixing bowl and mix carefully with the yeast. Add the remaining ingredients and work everything with a mixer (dough hook) briefly on the lowest, then on the highest level in about 5 minutes to a smooth dough.

3. Knead the dough briefly again on a lightly floured work surface. Roll out the dough into a square (35 x 35 cm). Place the butter square offset in the middle.

4. Fold the dough corners over so that the butter is wrapped. Roll out the dough and butter square into a rectangle (approx. 50 x 30 cm). The more precisely and precisely the dough is rolled out (since the butter is then evenly distributed in it), the more evenly it rises when baking.

5. Fold from the shorter sides towards the middle so that the edges of the dough meet, then fold the two sides together; 4 layers of dough are created. This is called a "double tour" Cover and place the dough in the refrigerator for 60 minutes.

6. Turn, roll out and fold the dough package in the same way as described above. Wrap in foil and place in the refrigerator for 60 minutes.

7. Cover the baking sheet with parchment paper.

8. Roll out the dough into a rectangle (60 x 50 cm) and cut in half so that you get 2 smaller rectangles (60 x 25 cm). Cut these rectangles into 4 rectangles (25 x 15 cm) and cut them in half diagonally so that triangles are created. Roll up the triangles from the broad side and bend them into "croissants". Place the croissants on the baking sheet with a little space between them and leave them covered again in a warm place for about 1 hour until they have visibly enlarged.

9. Preheat oven.

10. Top / bottom heat about 220 ° C

11. Hot air around 200 ° C

12. Beat the egg. Carefully brush the risen croissants with it and sprinkle with the seed mix as desired To bake.

13. After the first baking time, reduce the oven temperature and finish baking the croissants.

14. Top / bottom heating 200 ° C

15. Hot air 180 ° C

16. Baking time: 10 - 12 min

17. Put the croissants on a wire rack with the baking paper and let them cool.

PLUM JAM

Preparation time 30 minutes

Cooking / Baking time 1hour 20 minute minutes

Servings 2

INGREDIENTS

- ❖ 3 kg Plums (prepared weighed)
- ❖ 500 g sugar
- ❖ 2 pck Vanilla Sugar
- ❖ 1 tbsp Herb vinegar

PREPARATION

1. Prepare the plums
2. Wash and stone the plums and weigh 3 kg.
3. Let the juice steep
4. Place the fruit in a saucepan with the cut side down. Pour the weighed amount of sugar, bourbon vanilla sugar and herb vinegar over the plums and cover and chill overnight.
5. Bring the fruit mixture to a boil over medium heat and simmer in a closed saucepan over low heat for 2 hours, do not stir. Then simmer in the open pot for about 30 minutes, also do not stir. Then cook for another 20 minutes over high heat while stirring . Immediately fill the plum jam to the brim in prepared jars, close with screw lids (twist-off), turn over and leave on the lids for about 5 minutes.